Different Under God

The **Institute of Southeast Asian Studies (ISEAS)** was established as an autonomous organization in 1968. It is a regional research centre dedicated to the study of socio-political, security and economic trends and developments in Southeast Asia and its wider geostrategic and economic environment. The Institute's research programmes are the Regional Economic Studies (RES, including ASEAN and APEC), Regional Strategic and Political Studies (RSPS), and Regional Social and Cultural Studies (RSCS).

ISEAS Publishing, an established academic press, has issued more than 2,000 books and journals. It is the largest scholarly publisher of research about Southeast Asia from within the region. ISEAS Publishing works with many other academic and trade publishers and distributors to disseminate important research and analyses from and about Southeast Asia to the rest of the world.

Different Under God

A Survey of Church-going Protestants in Singapore

TERENCE CHONG
HUI YEW-FOONG

INSTITUTE OF SOUTHEAST ASIAN STUDIES
Singapore

First published in Singapore in 2013 by
ISEAS Publishing
Institute of Southeast Asian Studies
30 Heng Mui Keng Terrace
Pasir Panjang
Singapore 119614

E-mail: publish@iseas.edu.sg
Website: <http://bookshop.iseas.edu.sg>

ISEAS Library Cataloguing-in-Publication Data

Different under God : a survey of church-going Protestants in Singapore / by Terence Chong and Hui Yew-Foong.
1. Protestants—Singapore.
2. Church attendance—Singapore.
3. Christianity—Singapore.
I. Chong, Terence.
II. Hui, Yew-Foong.
BX4854 S6D56 2013

ISBN 978-981-4414-42-5 (soft cover)
ISBN 978-981-4414-43-2 (E-book PDF)

Typeset by International Typesetters Pte Ltd
Printed in Singapore by Chung Printing Pte Ltd

CONTENTS

ACKNOWLEDGEMENTS

This project would not have been possible without the support of different institutions and individuals. We are grateful to the Konrad-Adenauer-Stiftung, in particular to Dr Wilhelm Hofmeister, for supporting and funding this project. We would like to register our thanks to the Institute of Southeast Asian Studies for granting us the time to undertake the survey.

The support of the National Council of Churches of Singapore, as well as the kind encouragement of Bishop Dr Robert Solomon, was crucial to the successful execution of the survey. We also owe a debt to our able and indefatigable Project Manager, Jolynn Chew, who often went beyond the call of duty to ensure appointments, logistics and field assistants were well coordinated. Without her the project would not have run as smoothly. Gursharon Kaur Sidhu's research assistance was crucial to our data analysis.

At different stages of the project, we were privileged to have received advice and feedback from Dr Bobby Sng, Dr Irene Ng, Ms Neo Yu Wei, Pastor Colin Tan and Mr André J.M. De Winne, among others. In addition, this project would not have seen the light of day without the hospitality of the participating churches and its congregations. We are grateful for the goodwill they showed us.

Finally, although everyone acknowledged has contributed to the successful publication of this report in some way, the analyses and conclusions expressed hereforth are the responsibility of the authors.

INTRODUCTION

1. This survey is an attempt to tell a story of a complex community. It is a story of a community with very different members, many of whom come from different socio-economic backgrounds, sharing the same faith. As it is in many cases, the diversity within faith communities is often obscured, sometimes out of ignorance, sometimes out of political convenience, by the sheer visibility of religion and religiosity.

2. Christianity is one of the fastest growing religions in Singapore. According to Singapore census data, Singaporeans aged 15 years and over who professed to be Christians have grown from 14.6 per cent in 2000 to 18.3 per cent in 2010. In addition, it is a well educated community with over 40 per cent of a total of 350,000 Protestant Christians holding a university degree. Quite clearly, it is a story that needs to be told. This is not to say that the Christian community in Singapore has not been adequately studied. Indeed there have been several noteworthy local studies which have guided our thoughts and which we have duly cited in this report. However, the rapid growth of Christianity in Singapore has not been accompanied by systematic quantitative studies, unlike elsewhere (Putnam and Campbell 2010). As a result, many interesting qualitative arguments have not benefited from the broad overview that quantitative evidence provides.

3. The central plot to this story is the phenomenal growth of the so-called "megachurch" in Singapore.

Images of charismatic pastors, rock concert-like worship services and trendy congregations are certainly popular (see Ong 21 July 2008; Lee and Long 17 July 2010). But who are these megachurch members? What are their backgrounds? How do they view the world? How are they different from their Anglican or Methodist counterparts? On which issues do they converge? And while it is generally recognized that Protestant Christians in Singapore are mainly middle class (Clammer 1978, p. 2; Sng and You 1982, p. 59), are there variations within this middle class? And if so, do they correspond to denominations? These were the overarching questions that motivated this survey.

4. As we thought through these issues, it became clear that the megachurch was of sociological importance. It also became quickly evident that the megachurch could not be studied in isolation. Findings on the megachurch would have limited use if they could not be compared to mainline denominations or even smaller independent churches. As such, it was decided that the survey would cover Protestant Christians, specifically, megachurch-goers and the biggest Protestant communities in Singapore, namely the Anglicans, Methodists and independent church-goers. If given the choice, we would have liked to be as inclusive as possible. However, our exclusion of the Catholic community was the consequence of analytical tidiness as well as more mundane but very real constraints like time and funding limitations. In addition, although our survey included Bible-Presbyterians, the sample size was too small to be statistically significant and show reliable trends in comparison to other denominations. As such we have left them out of the charts.

5. With this comparative frame in mind, this survey seeks to understand the economic, social and cultural profiles of Protestant church-goers in Singapore. It also seeks to understand their attitudes toward certain public and social issues such as money and finance, politics, sex and sexuality, and perceptions of other faith and ethnic communities. It is precisely such data that is missing in the local literature on Christianity. Nevertheless, this survey is neither meant to be comprehensive nor the final word on the subject. It should be read as a broad sweep of the trends and patterns within the Protestant community. In highlighting such trends and patterns, this survey would serve, firstly, to support existing theses on the Christian community or to invite a re-think; and secondly, act as a springboard for follow-up studies of a more qualitative nature to be specifically designed.

6. There are, of course, limitations to surveys. For example, respondents may interpret questions differently from what was intended by the researcher. Through our pilot studies, we sought to find the best way to phrase questions and minimize such unintended interpretations. Surveys also do not tell us *why* people feel a certain way or do certain things. This is better answered by qualitative research. It may also be argued that individuals do not just have religious identities but are also citizens, parents, children, and would thus have a variation of perspectives to the same survey question depending on the situation they are in or the identity they take when the question is posed. Can such a survey then capture any individual's complexity? There are three qualifications we would like to raise. Firstly, no single survey can capture the multiple identities of an individual, and we certainly do not claim to do so. Secondly, this survey is only interested in our respondents' religious identity and not other social identities they may have, hence the undertaking of the survey in their church environment. Thirdly, it may be argued that religious identity is unlike any other in that it comes with moral dispositions which have a way of shaping one's worldview.

7. Readers will notice from the questionnaire sample in Annex One that we have left out Sections D and F. Readers will also notice that not all of the questions from other sections are included in the report. There are two reasons for this. Firstly, we left out findings that were not statistically significant. Secondly, for the sake of conciseness, we decided to include only the sections and questions that contributed to our understanding of the Protestant Christian middle class and its variations. Only data and findings that were pertinent to our hypotheses were included. This was more of an editorial decision to make the report more streamlined in advancing a coherent picture of the Protestant Christian community. This is not to say that we excluded data and findings that did not support our hypotheses. Indeed, by including findings that defied our initial assumptions such as the finding that megachurch-goers were less likely to be vocal about public policy issues forced us to think deeper and more profoundly about the community. The consequence, we believe, is a more complex portrait of our megachurch respondents.

8. Research into the Christian community in Singapore is fraught with the same politics and obstacles that come with researching any other community. As an outsider, the researcher may be initially viewed with some degree of suspicion while community leaders may be understandably protective of those under their charge. However, as any student of Singapore society knows, the particular history and socio-political context of the Christian community in relation to the state and other faith communities add another layer of politics that the researcher must grapple with. Historical awareness cannot be dispensed with. From the more labour-conscious Jurong Christian Church in the late 1960s, the so-called 'Marxist Conspiracy' in 1987, the passing of the Maintenance of Religious Harmony Act in 1990, the attempted takeover of a well known women's rights group in 2009, as well as several high profile cases of disparaging remarks about other faith communities, it is clear that the Christian community is constantly negotiating with the rest of society and with the state (see Chong 2011). While such negotiations are par for course in any multicultural and multireligious society, they sometimes give rise to sensitivities from within the community and do not make the job of sociologists and anthropologists any easier. Needless to say, we encountered our fair share of slammed doors.

9. We were open and honest with our intentions and motivations. We always introduced ourselves as researchers from the Institute of Southeast Asian Studies and actively sought out gatekeepers such as the National Council of Churches of Singapore and key church leaders in order to access the community. We were happy to share our questionnaire with any pastor who wanted, rightfully, to see the type of questions posed to his congregation beforehand. We were always amused and deeply gratified by the single most common reaction from church leaders upon examining our questionnaire: "Wow. Very interesting questions. I would also like to know the answers myself!" It is in the spirit of sharing and understanding that we produce this report.

Organization of Report

10. This introduction is followed by an "Executive Summary" that gives the reader a quick overview of our key findings. The "Findings, Analyses and Conclusions" section ties together our major conclusions within an analytical framework that builds the link between social differentiation and differentiation within the Protestant church. This is then followed by sections that describe our "Methodology" and the "Demographics of Respondents". Finally, the main body of the Report, the "Survey Findings", is where the reader will find detailed charts and figures.

EXECUTIVE SUMMARY

Introduction

11. This survey has two objectives. It seeks to understand the economic, social and cultural profiles of Protestant church-goers in Singapore. It also seeks to understand their attitudes toward certain public and social issues such as money and finance, politics, sex and sexuality, and perceptions of compatibility with other faith and ethnic communities.

12. This survey was conducted between December 2009 and January 2011 among 24 churches. A total of 2,663 questionnaires were analysed. The denominations included in the survey were the Anglicans, Methodists, Bible-Presbyterians, independent churches and megachurches.

Socio-economic and Cultural Background

13. The incomes of megachurch respondents tend to cluster around the middle level of $2,000 to $4,999, while mainline and independent church respondents are better represented at the extremes of the income spectrum, that is, those without income and those with income of $10,000 and above.

14. Megachurch respondents tend to come from a working class or lower middle class background, while mainline and independent church respondents tend to come from a middle class background.

15. In terms of housing type before the age of 18 for those aged 29 and below, megachurch respondents, at 19.0 per cent, were least likely to have lived in private housing. They were followed by Anglicans at 33.7 per cent, Independents at 39.3 per cent, and Methodists at 43.4 per cent.

16. For those aged 29 and below, megachurch respondents were least likely to have fathers with tertiary education, at 22.5 per cent, followed by Anglicans at 35.2 per cent, Independents at 39.8 per cent, and Methodists at 48.4 per cent.

17. For those aged 29 and below, megachurch respondents were least likely to have mothers with tertiary education, at 11.0 per cent, followed by Anglicans at 16.9 per cent, Independents at 25.3 per cent, and Methodists at 30.1 per cent.

18. In terms of the use of English at home before the age of 18 for those aged 29 and below, megachurch respondents have the lowest proportion at 71.7 per cent, followed by Independents at 71.9 per cent, Anglicans at 78.9 per cent, and Methodists at 88.6 per cent.

Reasons for Attending this Church

19. In terms of the context of conversion, megachurch respondents were most likely, at 53.0 per cent, to have been converted in their current church, and least likely, at 8.5 per cent, to have been born into a Christian family.

20. The highest ranked reasons for attending church do not differ much across denominations, with "teachings are doctrinally sound" and "deeper experience of God" being the most popular. The difference appears in the specific ranking order.

Money and Finance

21. Mainline and independent church respondents who tend to be older and with families were more likely to spend more of their income on "family expenses" while megachurch respondents, who tend to be younger with fewer family commitments, spent more on "personal expenses".

22. Megachurch respondents also allocated the highest amount of their income to church at 17.2 per cent. They were followed by Anglicans at 10.5 per cent, Independents at 9.9 per cent, and Methodists at 9.4 per cent.

23. One general trend found was that megachurch respondents were more likely to see a stronger relationship between giving to God and personal well-being. For example, they were more likely to agree (75.4 per cent) with the statement "By giving to my church I can expect God to bless me spiritually", compared to Anglicans at 38.7 per cent, and both Methodists and Independents at 35.8 per cent.

24. This trend was repeated in the response to the statement "By giving to my church I can expect God to bless me materially". Sixty-seven per cent of megachurch respondents agreed, followed by Independents at 19.4 per cent, Anglicans at 18.5 per cent, and Methodists at 17 per cent.

25. Another trend found was that megachurch respondents were less likely to compartmentalize market logic from spiritual matters or church organization. For example, 71.7 per cent of megachurch respondents agreed with the statement "The financial growth of my church is a sign of God's blessing over it". They were followed by Anglicans at 46.2 per cent, Methodists at 42 per cent, and Independents at 40 per cent.

26. This comparatively lower level of compartmentalization was also shown in the response to the statement "All full-time staff (e.g. Pastors, church workers, counsellors etc.) should be paid market-competitive salaries". Seventy-seven point six per cent of megachurch respondents agreed with the statement, followed by Independents at 44.8 per cent, Methodists at 42.3 per cent, and Anglicans at 39.8 per cent.

Politics

27. While megachurch respondents are as likely as respondents from mainline and independent churches to allow their Christian values to influence their views on public policies, they are less likely to view the moral character of public policy in Singapore with concern, and are also less likely to support intervening in public policy matters through the public sphere.

28. The majority of respondents across denominations agreed with the statement "My Christian values influence my views on public policy issues (e.g. casinos, abortion)". Megachurch respondents were the highest at 87.9 per cent, followed by Independents at 87.2 per cent, Methodists at 86.0 per cent, and Anglicans at 83.6 per cent.

29. Megachurch respondents, at 40.8 per cent, were least likely to agree with the statement "When it comes to public policies, the Singapore government is more concerned with economic benefits than with moral values". They were followed by Independents and Methodists, both at 60.3 per cent, and Anglicans at 62.2 per cent.

30. Megachurch respondents, at 33.3 per cent, were least likely to agree with the statement "Christians should collectively express their views on public policy issues in public". They were followed by Independents at 49.2 per cent, Anglicans at 52.1 per cent, and Methodists at 56.7 per cent.

Sex and Sexuality

31. Megachurch respondents are as conservative, if not more conservative, in comparison with respondents from mainline and independent churches with regard to values related to sex and sexuality. This is the case concerning pre-marital sex, the moral status of homosexuality and abortion. However, megachurch respondents are more likely to interact with and have friends who are homosexuals

32. The majority of respondents across denominations disagreed with the statement "Pre-marital sex (sex before marriage) is fine as long as those involved are consenting adults and if they practise safe sex". Megachurch respondents were the highest at 93.1 per cent, followed by Independents at 84.9 per cent, Methodists at 81.5 per cent, and Anglicans at 81.1 per cent.

33. The majority of respondents across denominations agreed with the statement "It is morally wrong to engage in homosexuality (same sex sexual relations)". Megachurch respondents were the highest at 85.7 per cent, followed by Methodists at 82.3 per cent, Independents at 81.5 per cent, and Anglicans at 79.7 per cent.

34. The majority of respondents across denominations agreed with the statement "Abortion is morally wrong". Megachurch respondents were the highest at 92.9 per cent, followed by Anglicans at 78.8 per cent, Independents at 77.1 per cent, and Methodists at 76.7 per cent.

35. Sixty-two point nine per cent of megachurch respondents have friends who are homosexuals, followed by 43.1 per cent of both Methodists and Independents, and 39.7 per cent of Anglicans.

36. Fifty-six point two per cent of megachurch respondents go out with friends who are homosexuals, followed by 32.2 per cent of Anglicans, 31.3 per cent of Methodists, and 31.0 per cent of Independents.

Other Religions and Communities

37. The conviction to spread the Gospel is strong across denominations. For example, in response to the statement "I believe God has commanded Christians to evangelise to everyone", 92.9 per cent of megachurch respondents agreed, followed by Independents at 91.3 per cent, Methodists at 89.8 per cent, and finally the Anglicans at 88.0 per cent.

38. This strong conviction may have, over time, reduced the levels of sensitivity towards others. The majority of respondents across denominations agreed with the statement "I believe that the message of God's Word can overcome ethnic and religious sensitivities in Singapore". Methodists were the highest at 78.4 per cent, followed by Anglicans at 77.8 per cent, megachurch respondents at 73.3 per cent, and finally Independents at 71.2 per cent.

39. This trend is repeated in the response to the statement "Unfriendly reactions from people of other religions are God's test of Christians' perseverance in spreading his Word". Here, 54.4 per cent of Anglican respondents agreed, followed by Methodists at 53.8 per cent, Independents at 45.7 per cent, and finally megachurch respondents at 35.7 per cent.

40. Megachurch respondents were more likely to have friends from different religions. Megachurch respondents were also (marginally) more likely to spend time with friends from different religions than respondents from other denominations.

FINDINGS, ANALYSES AND CONCLUSIONS

A Heterogeneous Middle Class Faith

41. The Protestant Christian community is a predominantly middle class community (Clammer 1978; Sng and You 1982). The Singapore middle class is, however, neither homogeneous nor static, and so too the case of the Protestant Christian community. The complex historical and political forces that have resulted in strong links between economic status and language proficiency in Singapore (Hill and Lian 1995; Kwok 2001) have also affected the Protestant Christian community, such that differentiation in social class and status are also reflected in the social organization of churches.

42. Generally speaking, the findings suggest that our respondents from the mainline denominations, as well as those from independent churches, are part of the established English-proficient middle class while megachurch-goers constitute part of the emergent middle class. Our Anglican, Methodist and independent church respondents were more likely to have better educated parents from more privileged socio-economic and English-speaking backgrounds, and lived in private property. These respondents were also more likely to have parents who are Protestant Christians. Meanwhile our megachurch respondents were more likely to have less educated parents, to have come from less privileged socio-economic and non-English-speaking backgrounds, and lived in public housing. They were also more likely to have parents who were non-Christians.

43. From this we can infer that our mainline and independent church respondents are more likely to have inherited their middle class status while our megachurch respondents are recent entrants into this class. Not only does this show the Singapore middle class to be dynamic, it also indicates that the transition from working or lower middle class backgrounds to middle class status makes the middle class a heterogeneous one in terms of perspectives and experiences.[1]

44. Although megachurch respondents are themselves as highly educated, if not more so, as our mainline and independent church respondents, the inherited class status of the latter suggests social distinction through cultural capital. According to Bourdieu (2002), economic class status is not the only way groups distinguish themselves from each other. Within broad communities such as the "middle class", the type of education, family background, language proficiency and lifestyle tastes — also known as cultural capital — create social distinction between groups. Such social distinctions may or may not be exhibited consciously or purposefully. These social distinctions and differences in cultural capital can be seen within the local Protestant Christian community in several ways.

Social Distinctions within the Community

45. Our Anglican, Methodist and independent church respondents were more likely to participate in civil society and advance their moral or political views publicly through civic discourse such as civil society or self-organization. They were more likely to be in favour of participating in the civic arena. This suggests a sense of confidence in their cultural capital as long-time members of the English-speaking middle class. Megachurch respondents, on the other hand, were less likely to do so. Through follow-up interviews, it was found that they preferred to express their moral or political views privately to friends or colleagues.

46. Another difference between Anglican, Methodist and independent church respondents, and megachurch respondents is in the practice of privatization and compartmentalization. The "compartmentalization and privatization" of religion occurs when the increased secularization of society leads an individual to compartmentalize her faith in order to negotiate the civic and public arena with greater ease (Bruce 2002; 2010). This may also result in the privatization of religion whereby one's faith becomes a private matter and is only shared with people of the same faith or those who show receptivity (Bruce 2002). In short, the distinctions between church and secular life, the spiritual and the material, the private and the public, believer and non-believer are made with greater clarity.

47. It was found that the denominations demonstrated selective compartmentalization and privatization over different issues. For example, we found that our megachurch respondents were more likely to demonstrate compartmentalization and privatization in matters such as moral and political views. As mentioned above, they were less likely to see civil society or public civic discourse as a means to express their moral or political views, preferring, instead, to keep such views private amongst friends and colleagues. In other words, megachurch respondents preferred to exercise moral influence through their private capacity in spheres that they were active in, rather than by imposing values through the church as a civic organization.

48. Conversely, our Anglican and Methodist respondents demonstrated less compartmentalization and privatization of their moral and political views as they, together with independent church respondents, were more likely to agree that Christians should collectively express their views on public policy issues in public. As implied above, this could be a function of confidence in the cultural capital they enjoy as members of the established middle class.

49. On the relationship between the material and the spiritual, the roles were reversed. It was found that megachurch respondents were more likely to see a stronger nexus between the material and the spiritual. Quantifiable criteria such as numerical and financial growth were more likely to be seen by megachurch respondents as signs of divine blessing and personal faithfulness. This is largely in keeping with the broader literature on the overlap of market logic and church organizational practices in megachurches (Twitchell 2004; Thumma and Travis 2007). However, it is unclear as to whether megachurch respondents see the *lack* of money or wealth as signs of a person's *lack* of faithfulness or *absence* of God's blessings. Conversely, our Anglican and Methodist respondents were more likely to see a separation between material and spiritual matters.

50. Why is there less evidence of compartmentalization and privatization between material and spiritual matters on the part of megachurch respondents? The penchant amongst megachurch respondents to use quantifiable criteria as indicators of spirituality and blessing suggests that megachurches express Christianity in the language of market ethos and logic, thus converging with and appealing to the economic aspirations and consumer habits of many young upwardly mobile Singaporeans. These young Singaporeans, in turn, not only find a brand of spirituality that is conducive in capitalist Singapore, but also familiarity with other Singaporeans of similar backgrounds undergoing the same class transitions. In sociological terms, this suggests that the ethos of the Singapore megachurch shares "elective affinity" (Weber 1991) with the aspirations of young upwardly mobile Singaporeans.

51. With regards to perception of other communities, the megachurch respondents were marginally higher than the mainline and independent church respondents in agreeing that their Christian values were compatible with other ethnic, cultural and religious communities in Singapore. Approximately one third of respondents were "neutral" on the matter suggesting that they did not have a strong opinion or that they preferred not to register a positive or negative answer. Nevertheless, megachurch respondents were more likely to have friends from different faith groups and to spend more of their leisure time with them. This, again, may be due to their non-Christian backgrounds as well as the "seeker church" orientation of many megachurches which encourages socializing with non-Christians in order to reach out to the contemporary world and to demonstrate the relevance of Christianity.

On Proselytization

52. On the issue of proselytization, we found that respondents across denominations, regardless of age and education, demonstrated strong convictions over the need to spread the Gospel. Nevertheless there were some denominational differences when it came to sensitivity. It was found that Anglican, Methodist and independent church respondents were less likely than megachurch respondents to be sensitive to unfriendly reactions from other faiths when proselytizing. This could be partly due to the former's inherited class status and cultural capital, as well as language barriers.

53. In contrast, megachurch respondents were more likely to be sensitive to unfriendly reactions from other faiths when proselytizing. A possible explanation for this is that megachurch respondents were more likely to have parents of non-Christian faiths. Having family members of non-Christian faiths and being more likely themselves to have converted from these faiths, together with greater proficiency in Mandarin or Chinese dialects, megachurch respondents may thus be more sensitized to how non-Christian faiths view Christian proselytization.

54. It was also found that there was a distinction between *conviction* over the need to proselytize and actual *follow-up action.* Post-survey interviews with respondents over the issue of proselytization revealed several qualifications. Some of their remarks include: "I'll only do it [evangelize] if the setting is right"; "Of course, I won't evangelize to a Muslim or someone whom I think is not receptive"; "We have to be sensitive to the setting"; "We can't just go up to a stranger and say 'do you want to accept Christ or not'... It's not going to work".

55. All these suggest that respondents may refrain from fully acting out their convictions for a variety of reasons. The socialization process from state institutions, national education and government discourse may have reinforced the message of the importance of religious harmony over decades, resulting in respondents mediating their actions to match social and cultural norms. In addition, respondents are reflexive agents who are able to rationally distinguish between private conviction and the possible ramifications of conviction-led actions. In such cases there is little follow-up action to this conviction.

56. However, post-survey interviews also reveal that respondents have adapted proselytization to the realities of the local multicultural setting. There may be three forms of *strategic proselytization*. A "friendship first" approach is where respondents may first befriend would-be converts before proselytizing. As one respondent remarked: "It is part of our 'caring system' where we show care and friendship first. We get to know them as real people first."

57. A "blessed persona" approach is where the Christian's personal life testimony is offered as an example of God's blessing in order to reach out to non-believers. By offering one's personal life as testimony, the respondent becomes a vivid demonstration of divine forgiveness, inclusion and happiness, thus making the abstract message of God's Word a tangible attraction for non-believers.

One respondent recounted: "People have asked me why I'm so happy, what secret do I have? Then I tell them."

58. Finally, the "opportune" approach is where respondents await the right opportunity to proselytize. Here, respondents approach people who they are familiar with such as fellow students or co-workers whom they think may be receptive to their message. They could be people facing personal crises, looking for meaning in life or whom they believe are ready to hear the message. In such cases, respondents rely on their own discretion and timing. One respondent remarked: "If they are Godless but happy, [I have] no problem! If they resist [the message of God] because they are down and unhappy, then wait for a while."

Conclusions

59. In conclusion, the Protestant Christian community, though predominantly middle class, is complex and dynamic. The trends and patterns found in the broader middle class are invariably reflected in the local Protestant Christian community. Such trends and patterns include the types of social distinction and cultural capital found between denominations. The relationship between economic position, social distinction and cultural capital, and denomination, is complex.

60. And while the Anglican, Methodist and independent church communities are themselves diverse, there is evidence that many of these respondents are members of the established middle class. Conversely, we can characterize megachurch respondents as the aspiring or emergent middle class that has achieved upward social mobility. The determination of the social class background of people who attend megachurches lends credence to the suggestion that megachurches succeed because they are able to articulate an ethos that is consonant with the values and experiences of an emergent middle class.

METHODOLOGY AND DEFINITIONS

61. The survey was administered to members of mainline denominations — namely the Anglican, Methodist and Bible-Presbyterian churches, as well as independent churches and megachurches.

62. Independent churches are defined here as churches that are not embedded within the organizational structure of any established denomination. The size of independent churches in this survey ranged from 120 to 800 sized congregations.

63. The literature defines a conventional "megachurch" as a Protestant church that draws weekly attendances of at least 2,000 or more (Thumma and Bird 2008). However, size alone does not define a megachurch. They are usually loosely tied to a mainline denomination or are non-denominational, and identify themselves as Pentecostal, evangelical or charismatic (Ellingson 2007). Typical megachurches in America witness weekly attendances of 20,000 or more. Meanwhile, in Singapore, the commonly understood notion of megachurch is that of non-mainline churches like New Creation, City Harvest, Faith Community Baptist Church, or The Lighthouse (see Ong 21 July 2002; Lee and Long 17 July 2010).

64. This survey — in the form of a questionnaire — was conducted with 24 churches from December 2009 to January 2011. A total of 2,860 questionnaires were returned, of which 2,663 were suitable for analysis.

65. Of the survey respondents, 579 (21.7 per cent) were from the Methodist church; 609 (22.9 per cent) were from the Anglican church; 66 (2.5 per cent) were from the Bible-Presbyterian church; 439 (16.5 per cent) were from independent churches; and 970 (36.4 per cent) were from the megachurches. While the sample from the Bible-Presbyterian church is included in the statistical analysis, their number is too small to be statistically significant and therefore they are not reflected in the charts. At the same time mainline churches, for analytical purposes in this study, will refer only to the Methodist and Anglican churches.

66. The questionnaire was subjected to two focus group discussions in order to ascertain the relevance of the questions. It was then referred to selected church leaders as well as the National Council of Churches of Singapore (NCCS) to ensure it did not offend sensitivities.

67. Two teams of Field Assistants were trained to administer the questionnaire as well as to answer any questions that respondents might have.

68. The preferred method of sampling — random sampling — was not an option for several reasons. Firstly, on a national level, there was no comprehensive list of Protestants in Singapore from which a random sample could be generated. Secondly, at the church level, many churches were understandably reluctant to randomly select and instruct their congregation members to partake in a survey while privacy considerations meant that we, as outsiders, could not undertake this task. Thirdly, the church member lists in some churches were not updated, resulting in discrepancies between the size of formal membership and weekly attendances.

69. Taking into consideration such limitations, we decided to employ multi-stage cluster sampling, whereby certain denominations and certain churches within denominations were invited to participate in this survey.

70. Great care was taken to ensure that the sampling was as representative as possible. For example, in the case of mainline denominations, church leaders were consulted over the selection of churches to ensure a broad socio-economic spectrum was achieved. To ensure linguistic and ethnic representation, English-, Mandarin- and Tamil-speaking congregations were also selected.

71. Upon the completion of the survey, two preliminary presentations of the general findings were made. The first was to the Executive Committee of NCCS. The purpose of this was to solicit feedback from the Executive Committee, which helped frame and refine research questions that were taken up at the post-survey focus group interviews. The second was to the church leaders of the participating churches.

The purpose was two-fold: to present to them a breakdown of the findings according to their own congregation, and to solicit feedback, which was considered in the post-survey focus group interviews.

72. In view of the feedback and certain trends regarding specific questions that differentiated the mainline from megachurch respondents that were discerned during the data analysing phase, we conducted two post-survey focus group interviews with megachurch respondents.

DEMOGRAPHICS OF RESPONDENTS[2]

Gender

73. Forty-four point eight per cent of the Christians surveyed were male, while 55.2 per cent were female (see Figure 1).

Figure 1
Census 2010 and Survey Respondents by Gender

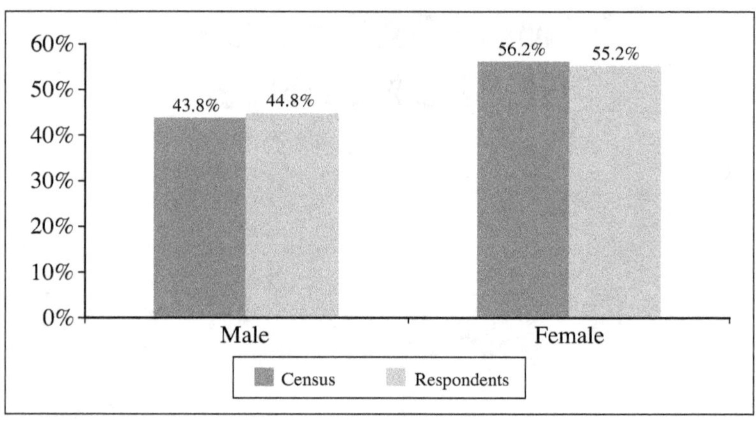

Nationality

74. Singaporeans made up 90.5 per cent of respondents, Permanent Residents made up 7.3 per cent, and foreigners made up 2.3 per cent.

Ethnicity

75. Respondents who identified themselves as "Chinese" made up 95.1 per cent, "Malay" 0.1 per cent, "Indian" 2.8 per cent, "Eurasian" 0.3 per cent, and "Others" 1.8 per cent (see Figure 2).

Figure 2
Census 2010 and Survey Respondents by Ethnicity

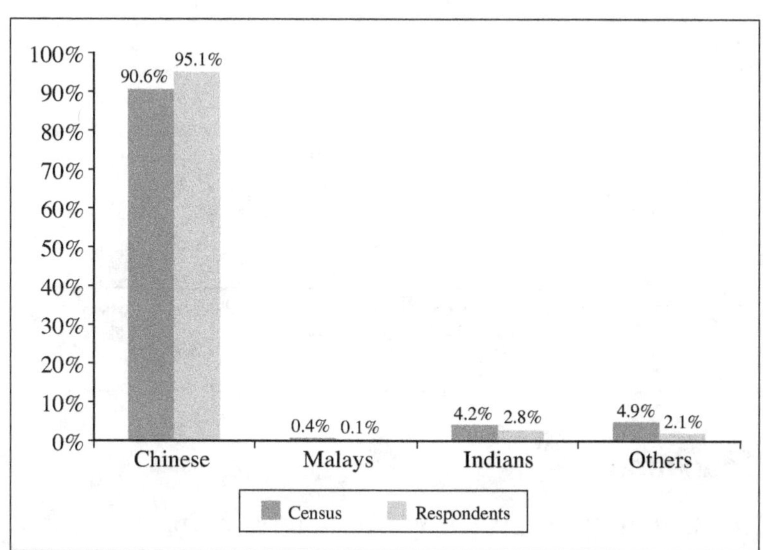

Age

76. Survey respondents aged between 18–29 years made up 36.2 per cent; 30–39 years — 20.75 per cent; 40–49 years — 20.06 per cent; 50–59 years — 16.05 per cent; 60 and above — 7.1 per cent. With the exception of the 18–29 group which was over-represented in the survey, and the 60 and above group which was under-represented, the rest of the age groups are proportionately similar to those of the broader national Christian community (see Figure 3).

Figure 3
Census 2010 and Survey Respondents by Age[3]

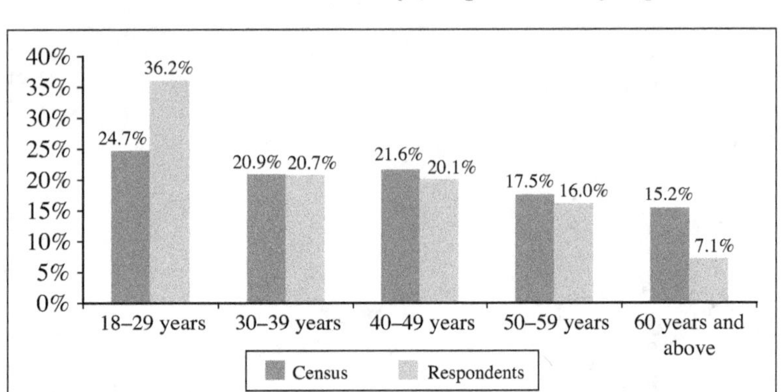

Education

77. Our sample is proportionately better educated than the national Protestant Christian population, according to Census 2010 data. Fifty-two point

Figure 4
Census 2010 and Survey Respondents by Education

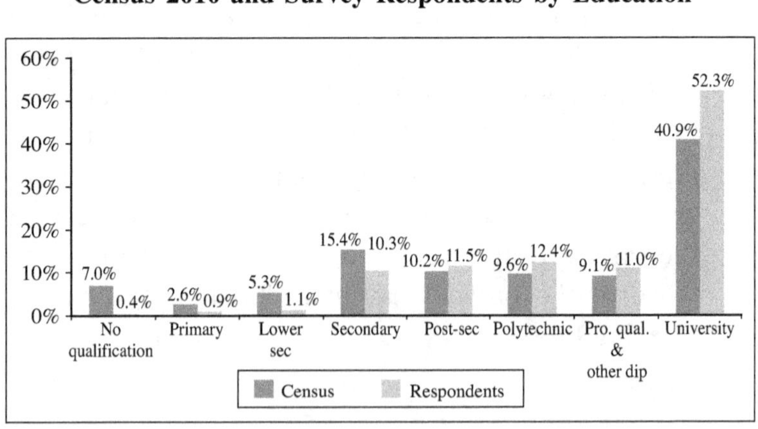

three per cent of respondents had at least university-level education, compared with 40.9 per cent at the national level (see Figure 4).

Marital Status

78. Forty-five point five per cent were single; 51.5 per cent were married; 1.8 per cent were divorced or separated; while 1.2 per cent were widowed (see Figure 5).

Figure 5

Census 2010 and Survey Respondents by Marital Status

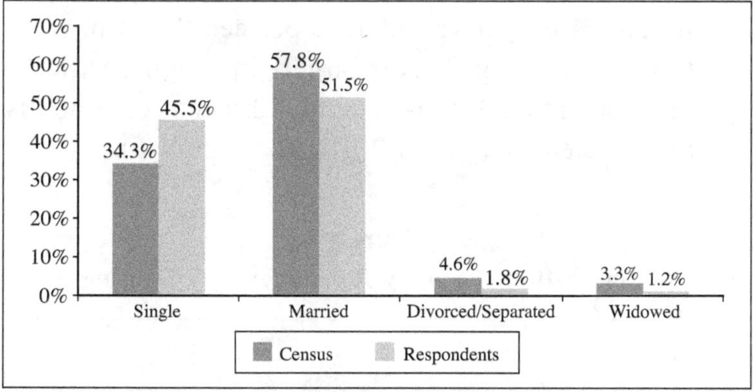

Schooling

79. Respondents of mainline denominations were likely to have attended primary and/or secondary schools of the same denomination. For example, 23 per cent of Methodists attended a Methodist primary school while 24.4 per cent of them attended a Methodist secondary school. Fourteen point four per cent of

Anglican respondents attended an Anglican primary school (10.8 per cent attended a Catholic primary school), while 24.1 per cent of them attended an Anglican secondary school (9.4 per cent attended a Catholic secondary school).

Housing

80. One point one per cent of respondents lived in 1–2 room flats; 10.6 per cent lived in 3-room flats; 23.16 per cent lived in 4-room flats; 30.85 per cent lived in 5-room flats; 18.24 per cent lived in condominiums and private flats; 14.2 per cent lived in landed property; and 1.82 per cent lived in other types of housing. This is largely in keeping with the broader national non-Catholic Christian community as reflected in Census 2010 (see Figure 6).

Figure 6

Census 2010 and Survey Respondents by Housing

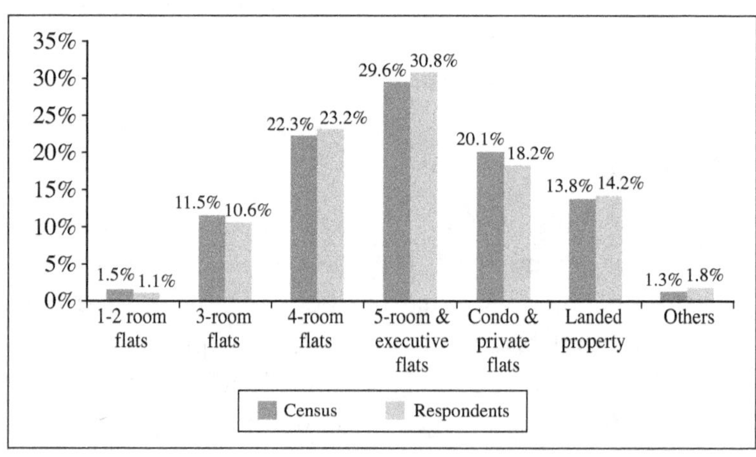

SURVEY FINDINGS

Section A: Socio-economic and Cultural Background

81. The questions in this section seek to define social differentiation in both socio-economic and cultural terms. Socio-economic variables include factors such as income levels and housing. Cultural variables include factors such as educational levels and language used at home. In seeking to understand socio-economic status in inter-generational terms, this section also delves into the socio-economic and cultural background of respondents' parents. The purpose is to find out if there are significant differences in class status and background between members of different denominations. Where possible, a chi-square test of independence was performed to determine whether there was a significant relationship between the variables.

82. The gross monthly personal income categories we have selected are: no income, $1,999 and below, $2,000 to $4,999, $5,000 to $9,999 and $10,000 and above. The second and third categories accord with the 1st to 50th percentile and 51st to 90th percentile of average monthly income per household member in 2010 respectively (Department of Statistics 2011, p. 12).

83. For the sample surveyed, 15.4 per cent of respondents have no income, 18.8 per cent earn $1,999 and below per month, 38.7 per cent earn from $2,000 to $4,999 per month, 17.8 per cent earn from $5,000 to $9,999

Figure A3-1
Breakdown by Income Categories

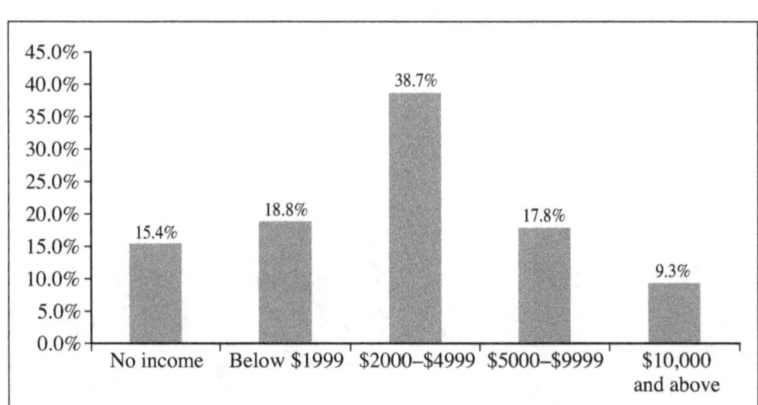

per month and 9.3 per cent earn $10,000 and above per month (see Figure A3-1).

84. When income levels are compared across denominations, the general trend is that mainline and independent churches are better represented at the extremes of the income spectrum, whereas megachurch respondents' incomes cluster around the middle level.

85. For the category of respondents with no income, mainline churches and independent churches have slightly higher proportions in comparison with megachurches. While 11.4 per cent of megachurch respondents have no income, 20.3 per cent of Methodists, 15.9 per cent of Anglicans and 17.3 per cent of Independents are found in the same category (see Figure A3-2).

Figure A3-2
Income Category by Denomination

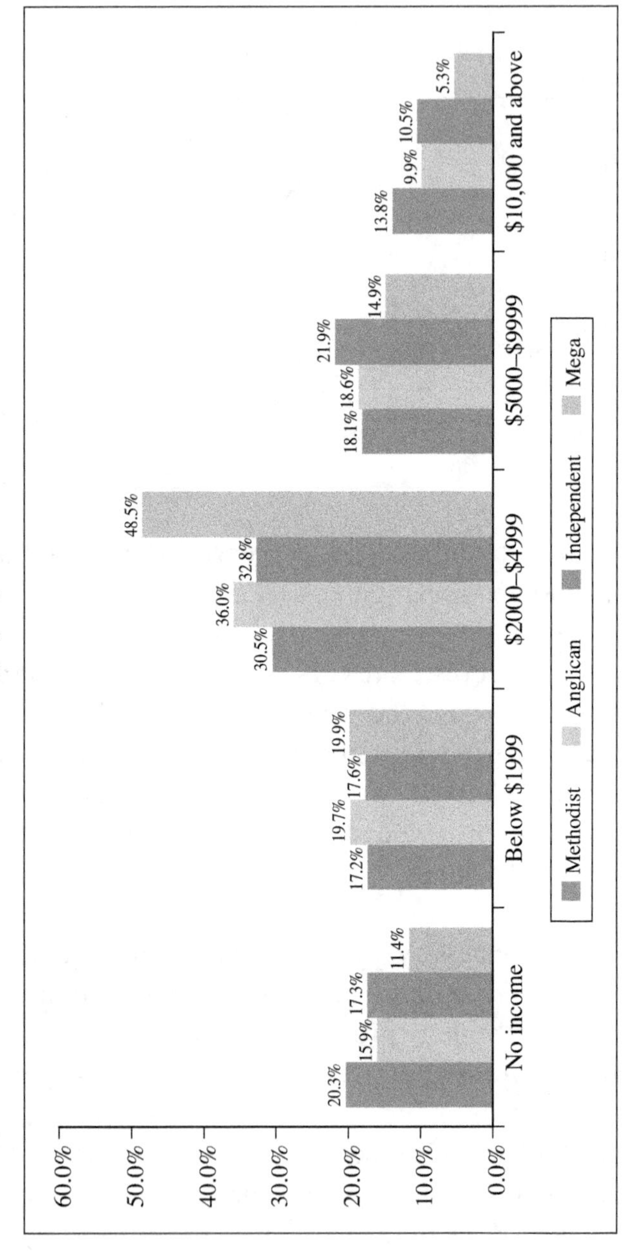

The relation between the variables is significant, X^2 (16, N = 2582) = 107.924, p = .000 (an alpha level of .05 was adopted for this and all subsequent statistical tests).

86. At the higher income levels, megachurch respondents are less well represented. Only 14.9 per cent of megachurch respondents fall into the $5,000 to $9,999 income bracket, whereas 18.1 per cent of Methodists, 18.6 per cent of Anglicans and 21.9 per cent of Independents earn this income level. For the highest monthly income level of $10,000 and above, only 5.3 per cent of megachurch respondents fall into this category, whereas 13.8 per cent of Methodists, 9.9 per cent of Anglicans and 10.5 per cent of Independents are in this income category.

87. On the other hand, megachurch respondents are significantly better represented in the middle income tier. Thus, while 48.5 per cent of megachurch respondents earn from $2,000 to $4,999, only 30.5 per cent of Methodists, 36.0 per cent of Anglicans and 32.8 per cent of Independents are found in the same income category in comparison.

88. As this disparity in income levels may be the result of younger respondents (aged 29 and below) being over-represented in the megachurches' sample, cross-tabulations for denomination and income level was made by controlling for age group i.e. 29 years and below and 30 years and above.

89. It is found that most of those earning $5,000 and above are in the 30 years and above age group.

Figure A3-3
Income Category by Denomination, Aged 30 and Above

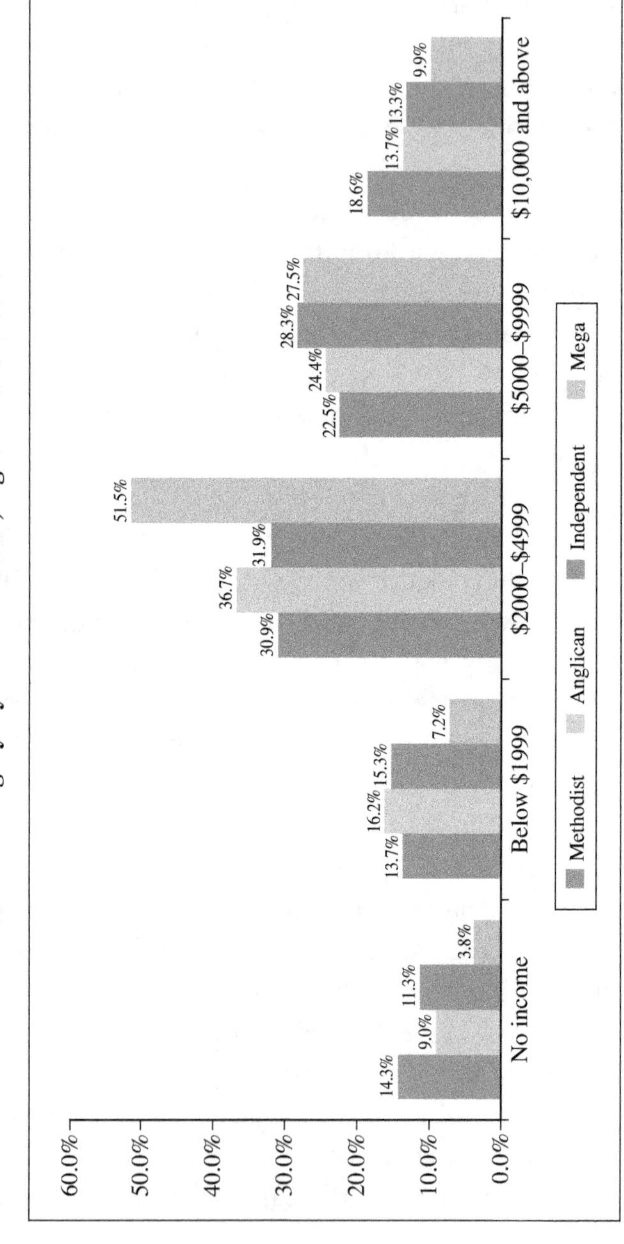

The relation between the variables is significant, X^2 (16, N = 1532) = 91.011, p = .000.

Within this age group, representation in the $5,000 to $9,999 income category among denominations is comparable. Twenty-two point five per cent of Methodists, 24.4 per cent of Anglicans, 28.3 per cent of Independents and 27.5 per cent of megachurch respondents aged 30 years and above are found in this income category. For the $10,000 and above income category, however, megachurch respondents are less well represented. While 18.6 per cent of Methodists, 13.7 per cent of Anglicans and 13.3 per cent of Independents are found in this income category, only 9.9 per cent of megachurch respondents are found in the same income category (see Figure A3-3).

90. However, across the age groups, megachurch respondents still cluster around the middle income level, as compared to respondents from other denominations. For those aged 29 years and below, 46.2 per cent of megachurch respondents are earning $2,000 to $4,999, while only 31.8 per cent of Methodists, 33.3 per cent of Anglicans and 28.7 per cent of Independents are found in the same income category (see Figure A3-4). As for those aged 30 and above, 51.5 per cent of megachurch respondents are earning $2,000 to $4,999, while only 30.9 per cent of Methodists, 36.7 per cent of Anglicans and 31.9 per cent of Independents are found in the same income category (see Figure A3-3).

Figure A3-4
Income Category by Denomination, Aged 29 and Below

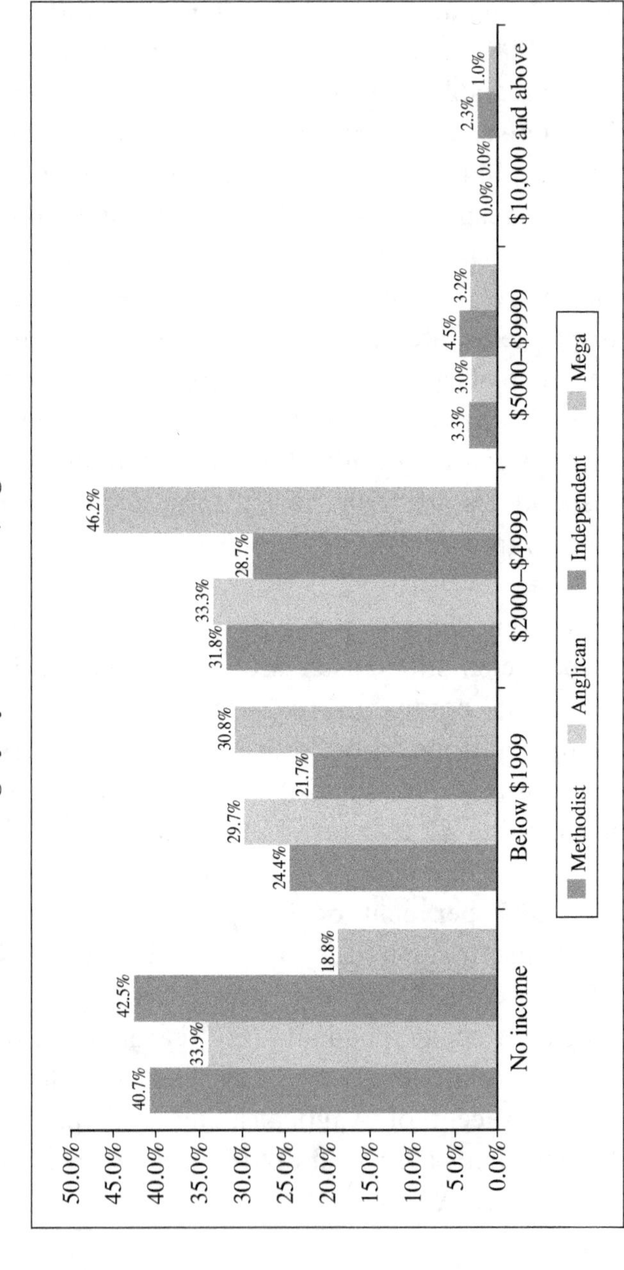

The relation between the variables is significant, X^2 (16, N = 884) = 52.779, p = .000.

91. At the same time, across age groups, there are proportionately fewer megachurch respondents in the no income category. For those aged 29 years and below, 40.7 per cent of Methodists, 33.9 per cent of Anglicans and 42.5 per cent of Independents profess to have no income, while only 18.8 per cent of megachurch respondents have no income. For this age group, these respondents without income are likely to be students and, to a lesser extent, housewives. For those aged 30 years and above, 14.3 per cent of Methodists, 9.0 per cent of Anglicans and 11.3 per cent of Independents profess to have no income, while only 3.8 per cent of megachurch respondents have no income. For this age group, these respondents without income are likely to be retirees and, to a lesser extent, housewives.

92. However, to have larger proportions of members in the no income category does not necessarily mean that these members are situated in more economically challenging conditions. On the contrary, the greater likelihood is that members of mainline and independent churches, especially those aged 29 and below, have better socio-economic backgrounds than members of megachurches, such that they can afford to have no incomes.

93. To determine more clearly the socio-economic background of respondents aged 29 years and below, we now turn to questions about housing before the age of 18.

94. A11 *What kind of housing did you stay in the longest before the age of 18?*

In asking about the kind of housing the respondent stayed in before the age of 18, the assumption is that the property was owned by the respondent's parent(s), and as such is an indicator of the socio-economic background of the respondent.

For those aged 29 years and below, it is found that the majority of megachurch respondents — 79.6 per cent — had stayed in public housing[4] before the age of 18, as compared with 54.0 per cent of Methodists, 66.3 per cent of Anglicans and 58.4 per

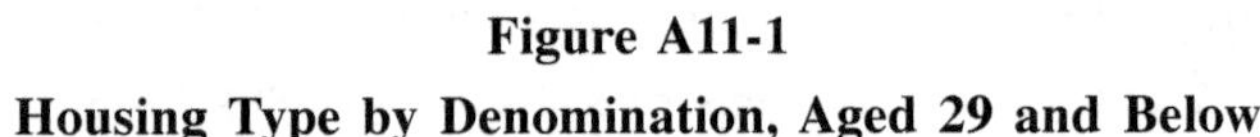

Figure A11-1
Housing Type by Denomination, Aged 29 and Below

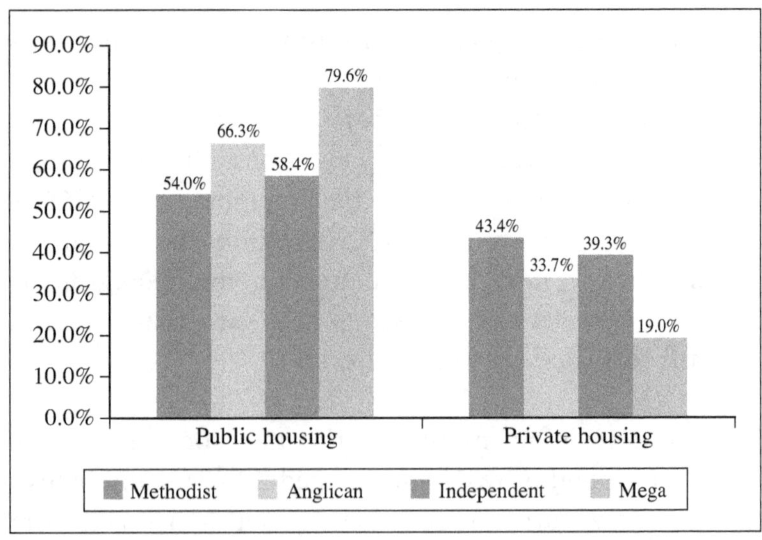

The relation between the variables is significant, $X^2(8, N = 885) = 51.949, p = .000$.

cent of Independents. In terms of private housing,[5] only 19.0 per cent of megachurch respondents had stayed in such housing before the age of 18, as compared with 43.4 per cent of Methodists, 33.7 per cent of Anglicans and 39.3 per cent of Independents (see Figure A11-1).

95. Thus, for those aged 29 years and below, those attending mainline and independent churches tend to have better socio-economic background as compared with those attending megachurches, when we consider housing before the age of 18 as an indicator.

96. Another form of social differentiation is to be found in the cultural background of respondents. Certain aspects of a person's cultural background, usually associated with parents, can lead to the transmission of attitudes and knowledge that help him or her succeed in the educational system. This is usually known in sociology as "cultural capital" (Bourdieu 1986; Bourdieu and Passeron 1977). In this survey, we sought to measure cultural capital through the highest level of education attained by respondents, the highest level of education attained by respondents' parents and the language used at home before the age of 18.

97. While the educational level attained is the most direct measure of a respondent's cultural capital, the educational level of parents also play a significant role in the socialization of the respondent for educational success. At the same time, in the context of Singapore, where English is the main medium of instruction in schools, the use of English in the home will also give respondents an advantage in achieving success in the education system (Chew 2007, pp. 74–79). To avoid skewing of the data due to the over-representation of respondents aged 29 years and below, especially in the megachurch sample, our analysis for cultural capital will focus only on those aged 29 years and below.

98. A1 *What is the highest level of education that you have attained?*

Fifty point two per cent of megachurch respondents have at least a university first degree or university postgraduate diploma or degree, followed by 44.9 per cent of Independents, 42.8 per cent of Anglicans and 36.6 per cent of Methodists. As for polytechnic diploma, 24.5 per cent of megachurch respondents have attained this level of education, followed by 21.3 per cent of Independents, 16.3 per cent of Anglicans and 12.2 per cent of Methodists. At the prima facie level, it appears that megachurch respondents aged 29 and below are better educated than respondents from mainline and independent churches (see Figure A1-1).

Figure A1-1

Education Level by Denomination, Aged 29 and Below

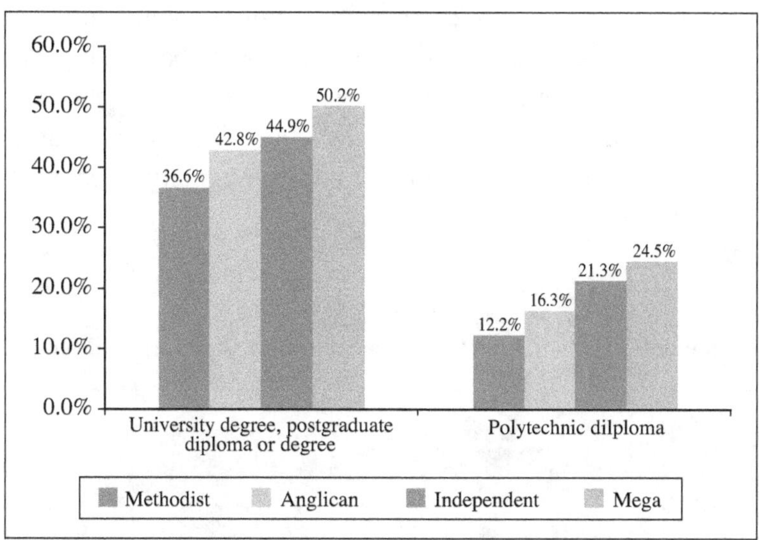

The relation between the variables is significant, X^2 (8, N = 889) = 40.283, p = .000.

99. A6 *What is your father's highest educational qualification?*

Megachurch respondents have the highest proportion of fathers with no formal schooling, or with primary or secondary education, at 64.0 per cent, followed by Anglicans at 43.6 per cent, Independents at 43.2 per cent and Methodists at 34.4 per cent. As for fathers with pre-university education, megachurch respondents have the lowest proportion at 12.7 per cent, followed by Methodists at 16.4 per cent, Independents at 17.0 per cent and Anglicans at 21.2 per cent. Megachurch respondents also have the lowest proportion for fathers with tertiary education at 22.5 percent, followed by Anglicans at 35.2 per cent, Independents at 39.8 per cent and Methodists at 48.4 per cent. As such, we can infer that respondents from mainline and independent churches have better educated fathers than respondents from megachurches (see Figure A6-1).

Figure A6-1
Father's Education Level by Denomination, Aged 29 and Below

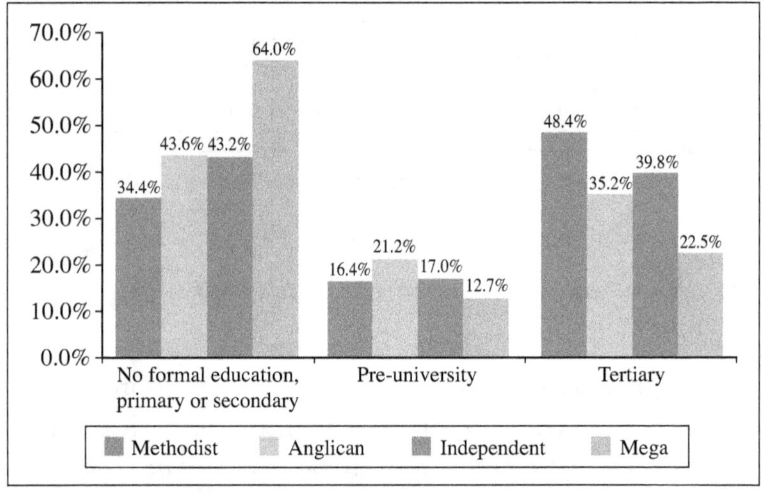

The relation between the variables is significant, X^2 (12, N = 886) = 61.718, p = .000.

100. A7 *What is your mother's highest educational qualification?*

Megachurch respondents have the highest proportion of mothers with no formal schooling or with primary education, at 30.7 per cent, followed by Independents at 17.2 per cent, Anglicans at 13.3 per cent and Methodists at 13.0 per cent. As for mothers with secondary education, Anglicans have the highest proportion at 48.8 per cent, followed by megachurch respondents at 44.0 per cent, Independents at 37.9 per cent and Methodists at 35.0 per cent. When it comes to mothers with pre-university education, megachurch respondents have the lowest proportion at 14.1 per cent, followed by Independents at 19.5 per cent, Anglicans at 21.1 per cent and Methodists at 22.0 per cent. Megachurch respondents also have the lowest proportion for mothers with tertiary education at 11.0 per cent, followed by Anglicans at 16.9 per cent, Independents at 25.3 per cent and Methodists at 30.1 per cent. As such, we can infer that respondents from mainline and independent churches have better educated mothers than respondents from megachurches (see Figure A7-1).

101. A5 *What language(s) did you use at home before the age of 18?*

As 96.8 per cent of respondents are Chinese, the more significant data on language use at home relates to the use of English and Mandarin. The Methodists have the highest proportion of English speakers at home, at 88.6 per cent, followed by Anglicans at 78.9 per cent, then Independents at 71.9 per cent and megachurch respondents at

Figure A7-1

Mother's Education Level by Denomination, Aged 29 and Below

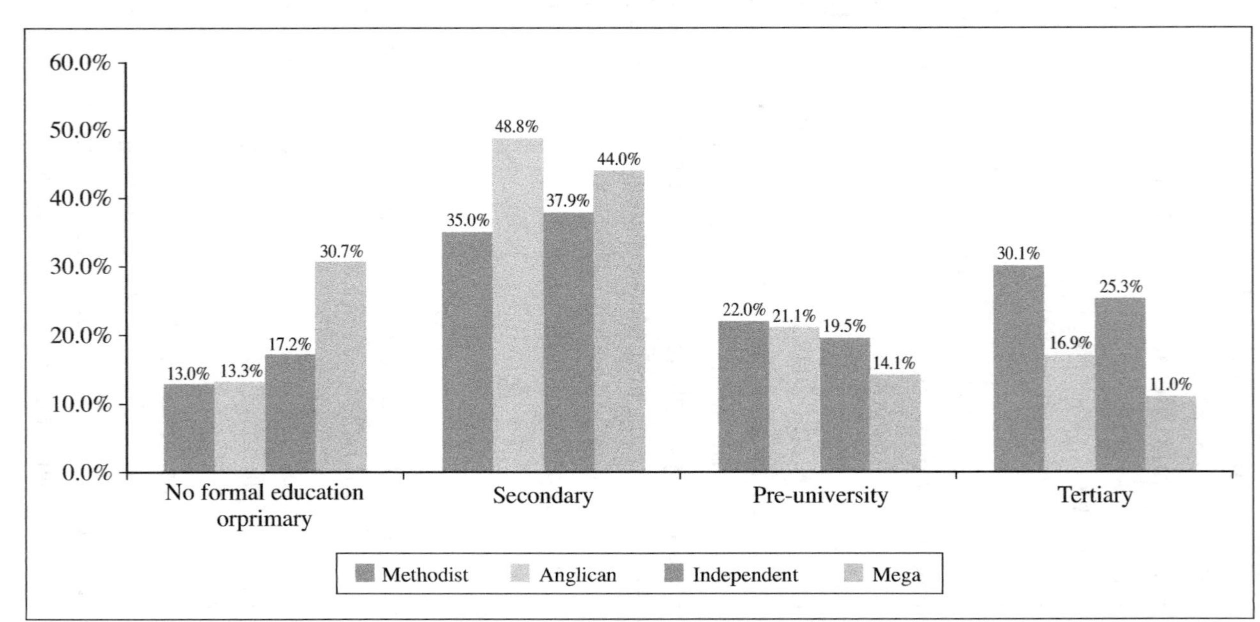

The relation between the variables is significant, X^2 (16, N = 887) = 69.274, p = .000.

71.7 per cent. As for Mandarin speakers at home, megachurch respondents have the highest proportion at 75.3 per cent, followed by Independents at 64.0 per cent, Anglicans at 59.0 per cent and Methodists at 51.2 per cent. As such, respondents from mainline churches are more likely to have used English at home as compared to respondents from independent and megachurches. On the other hand, megachurch respondents are more likely to have used Mandarin at home, as compared to respondents from independent and mainline churches (see Figure A5-1).

Figure A5-1
Language Use At Home Before Age of 18 by Denomination, Aged 29 and Below

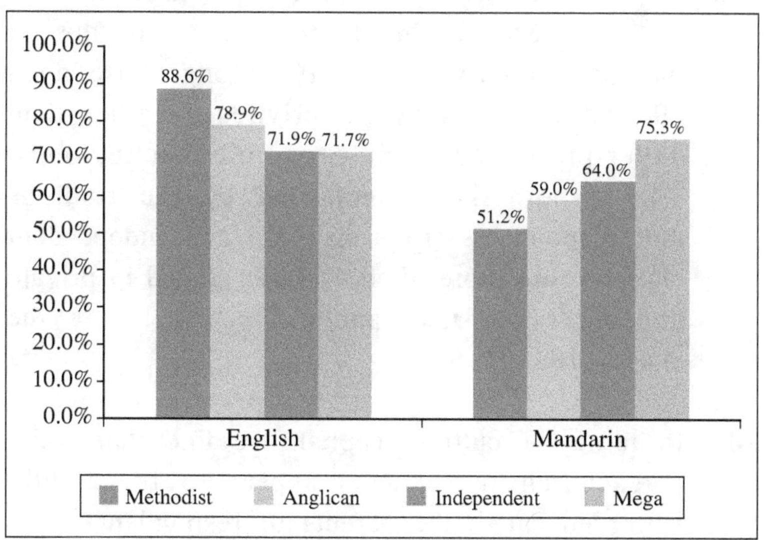

Conclusion

102. While this section sought to measure the socio-economic status of respondents, it also placed emphasis on determining the socio-economic background of respondents. In terms of income, megachurch respondents tend to cluster around the middle-tier, while mainline and independent church respondents are more evenly distributed among the different income categories. However, the fact that mainline and independent church respondents are better represented in the highest and no income categories may actually suggest that they are, in general, more affluent or have better socio-economic backgrounds than megachurch respondents.

103. In particular, the higher representation of mainline and independent church respondents in the no income category, especially among those aged 29 and below, suggests privileged rather than under-privileged socio-economic backgrounds. This hypothesis is supported by the findings that respondents from mainline and independent churches are more likely to have stayed in private housing rather than public housing before the age of 18.

104. In terms of cultural capital, we find that while megachurch respondents appear to be slightly better educated, the parents of respondents from mainline and independent churches are much better educated. In addition, respondents from mainline and independent churches are more likely to have used English at home before the age of 18.

105. Conversely, megachurch respondents aged 29 and below are more likely to have lived in public housing, spoken Mandarin at home, and have parents with lower levels of education. In spite of the more predominantly working class or lower middle class background, these respondents nevertheless were able to attain high levels of education and earn middle level incomes.

106. In other words, we can characterize megachurch respondents as the aspiring or emergent middle class that has achieved upward social mobility. The determination of the social class background of people who attend megachurches lends credence to the suggestion that megachurches succeed because they are able to articulate an ethos that is consonant with the values and experiences of an emergent middle class (Tong 2008, pp. 197–99; Ellingson 2010, pp. 254–55).

Section B: Reasons for Attending this Church

107. This section seeks, first, to determine the patterns of conversion and the movements between churches. Secondly, we seek to find out the reasons that attract Christians to the different churches.

108. B1.2 *Where did you convert?*

In response to this question, most respondents were born into a Christian family (17.8 per cent), converted at the current church (36.8 per cent) or converted at another church (20.0 per cent). Smaller proportions were converted at mass evangelistic rallies (4.5 per cent), at the activities of para-church organizations (5.7 per cent) or schools (6.0 per cent) (see Figure B1.2-1).

Mainline churches were more likely to have respondents born into Christian families as compared with respondents from independent and megachurches. Twenty-nine point two per cent of Anglicans and 26.4 per cent of Methodists were born into Christian families, followed by 10.7 per

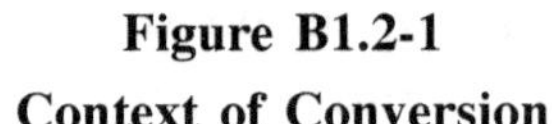
Figure B1.2-1
Context of Conversion

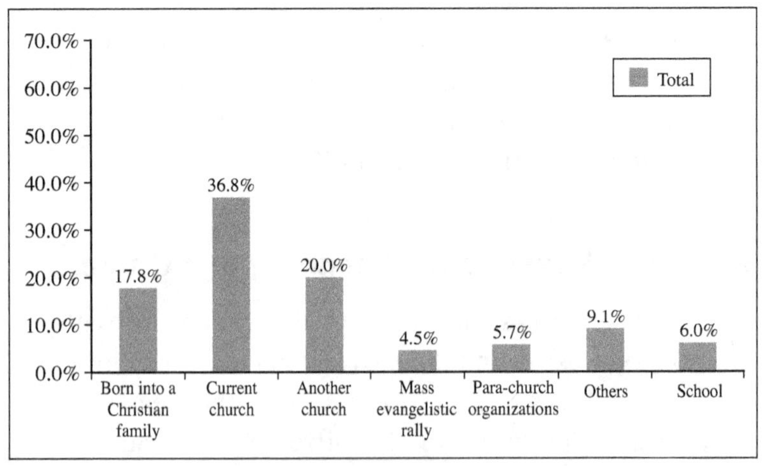

cent of Independents and 8.5 per cent of megachurch respondents.

Megachurches are most likely to have respondents converted at their churches, at 53.0 per cent, followed by Anglicans at 30.9 per cent, Independents at 28.5 per cent and Methodists at 24.3 per cent. On the other hand, independent churches are most likely to have respondents who were converted at another church, at 28.8 per cent, followed by Methodists at 18.7 per cent, megachurch respondents at 18.2 per cent and Anglicans at 17.2 per cent (see Figure B1.2-2).

Figure B1.2-2
Context of Conversion by Denomination

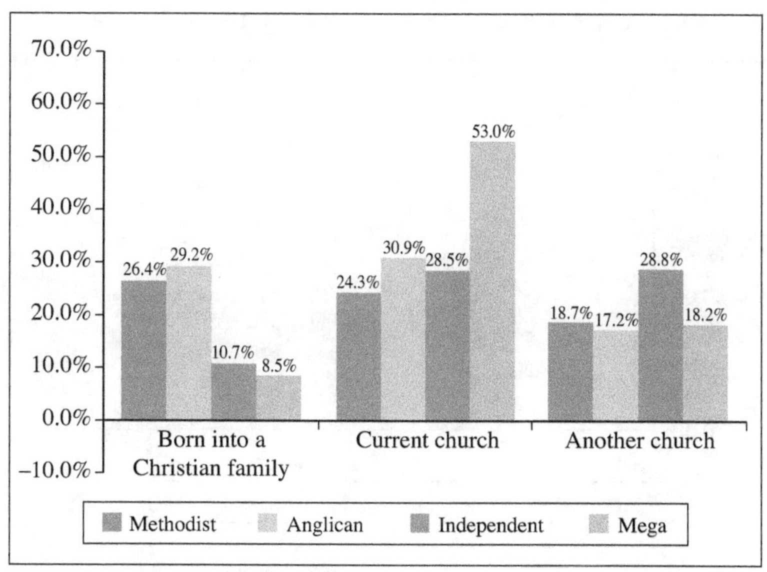

The relation between the variables is significant, X^2 (24, N = 2646) = 315.966, p = .000.

109. B2 *Is your current church the first church you have attended since you became a Christian?*

Fifty-seven point five per cent of megachurch respondents answered "yes" to this question, followed by 55.9 per cent of Anglicans, 48.8 per cent of Methodists and 35.3 per cent of Independents (see Figure B2).

110. Respondents who answered "no" were further asked to list the churches they had regularly attended (for at least six months) since they became Christians. For mainline churches, significant proportions of respondents had come from churches

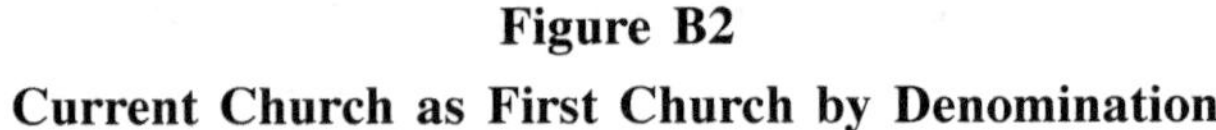

Figure B2
Current Church as First Church by Denomination

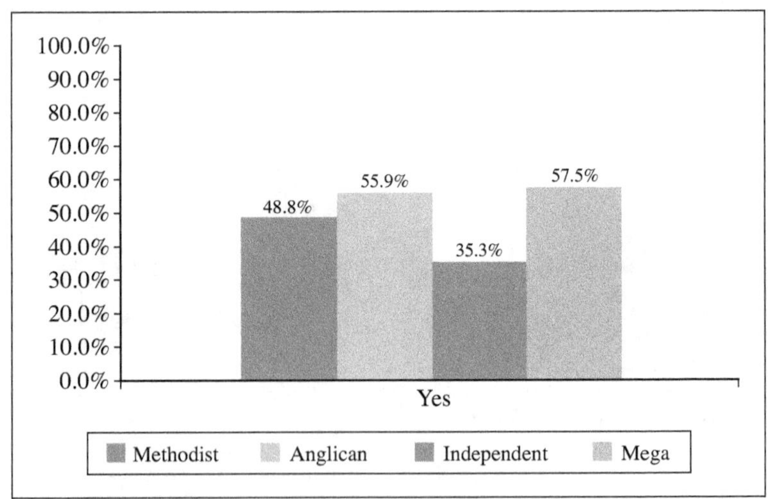

The relation between the variables is significant, X^2 (4, N = 2640) = 74.207, p = .000.

within their respective denominations. That is, for the Methodists, 18.0 per cent had come from other Methodist churches, and for the Anglicans, 12.5 per cent had come from other Anglican churches. For Independents, higher proportions of respondents who had come from other churches came from megachurches (15.3 per cent) and Methodist churches (14.1 per cent). As for megachurches, higher proportions of respondents from other churches came from Methodist churches (8.1 per cent) and Assembly of God churches (7.1 per cent).

111. To explore the main reasons why respondents attended their churches, respondents were asked to respond to 5-point Likert items associated with different reasons for attending their current churches. These reasons include:

i) I have always attended this church.
ii) I like the preaching.
iii) The teachings are doctrinally sound.
iv) I like the small group ministry.
v) I have made good friends here.
vi) I like the activities/programmes of this church.
vii) I have a deeper experience of God here.
viii) I feel the Word of God is lived out here.
ix) I feel that the people in this church care for me.
x) I like the praise and worship sessions.
xi) My parent(s) attend this church.
xii) It is an exciting church.
xiii) It is a big church.

112. If we consider only the "strongly agree" responses and rank the reasons, there are significant overlaps in the top-ranked reasons across denominations, although there are also distinctive patterns that are discernible. For the mainline churches, the four highest ranked reasons are, namely, "teachings are doctrinally sound", "always attended this church", "good friends" and "deeper experience of God". The highest ranked reasons for Independents are "teachings are doctrinally sound", "Word of God is lived out here", "deeper experience of God" and "preaching". As for megachurch respondents, the highest ranked reasons are "deeper experience of God", "Word of God is lived out here", "teachings are doctrinally sound" and "preaching".

Reasons for attending church

Rank	Mainline churches	Independent churches	Megachurches
1.	teachings are doctrinally sound	teachings are doctrinally sound	deeper experience of God
2.	always attended this church	Word of God is lived out here	Word of God is lived out here
3.	good friends	deeper experience of God	teachings are doctrinally sound
4.	deeper experience of God	preaching	preaching

Conclusion

113. In comparison with the mainline churches and megachurches, independent churches have a larger proportion of respondents who were originally from other churches. This is due, partly, to lower rates of conversion in comparison with the megachurches. At the same time, independent churches also experience lower rates of attendees who were born into Christian families.

114. Significantly, among reasons for attending their current church, "always attended this church" ranks highly among mainline church respondents, which suggests that there is a "habitual" element to the motivation behind attending church. This is not surprising given that mainline churches have higher rates of respondents born into Christian families.

115. Also significantly, what megachurch respondents rank highly as reasons for attending their church is not different from what other denominations would rank highly. The reasons generally thought of as attracting people to megachurches, or as key factors to church growth (Thumma and Travis 2007), such as "praise and worship", "exciting church", "people care for me" and "small group ministry", are ranked 5th, 6th, 7th and 8th respectively. The size of the megachurch, which Goh (2008, p. 302) argues serves to embody the experience of an infinite God, ranks near the bottom of the list at 12th. It can be argued that although these reasons do not rank near the top, they contribute to what megachurch respondents would consider a "deeper experience of God". However, more research will have to be done beyond this survey to ascertain the validity of such a hypothesis.

Section C: Money and Finance

116. According to the scholarly literature on megachurches, many American megachurches combine highly intense personal religiosity with contemporary cultural relevance by appropriating the aesthetic and media technologies of pop culture (Miller 1997; Sargeant 2000). Specifically, it has been argued that these megachurches employ corporate marketing practices, consumerist logic and neo-capitalist strategies to boost their growth and recruitment rates (Elisha 2004; Ellingson 2010).

117. This section has two objectives. Firstly and broadly, it seeks to gauge the respondents' general attitudes towards money management, and secondly, it attempts to contribute to the literature on megachurches by gauging the differences, if any, in attitudes towards market logic and church organization between mainline and megachurch respondents.

118. Respondents were asked how they allocated their income according to five categories. For Methodists, Independents and Anglicans, the highest expenditure came from "family expenses", followed by "personal expenses", "savings", "others" and finally "giving to church".

119. For megachurch respondents, however, the highest expenditure came in the form of "personal expenses", followed by "family expenses", "savings", "giving to church" and finally "others". Of all the respondents, megachurch respondents gave the highest percentage to church — 17.22 per cent — while the rest gave between 9–10 per cent (see Figure C1).

120. C2.1 *Money is important to me*

Most respondents agreed that money was important to them. Sixty-six per cent of them answered "agree" or "strongly agree", while 26.9 per cent were "neutral" and 7.2 per cent answered "disagree" or "strongly disagree". In terms of denomination breakdown, megachurch respondents were more likely to agree that money was important to them. Seventy-nine point four per cent of them answered "agree" or "strongly agree", compared to 62.1 per cent of Methodists or 55.4 per cent of Anglicans. This may be due to the fact that megachurch respondents are more likely to be socially upwardly mobile, hence attaching more

Figure C1
Income Allocation According to Denomination

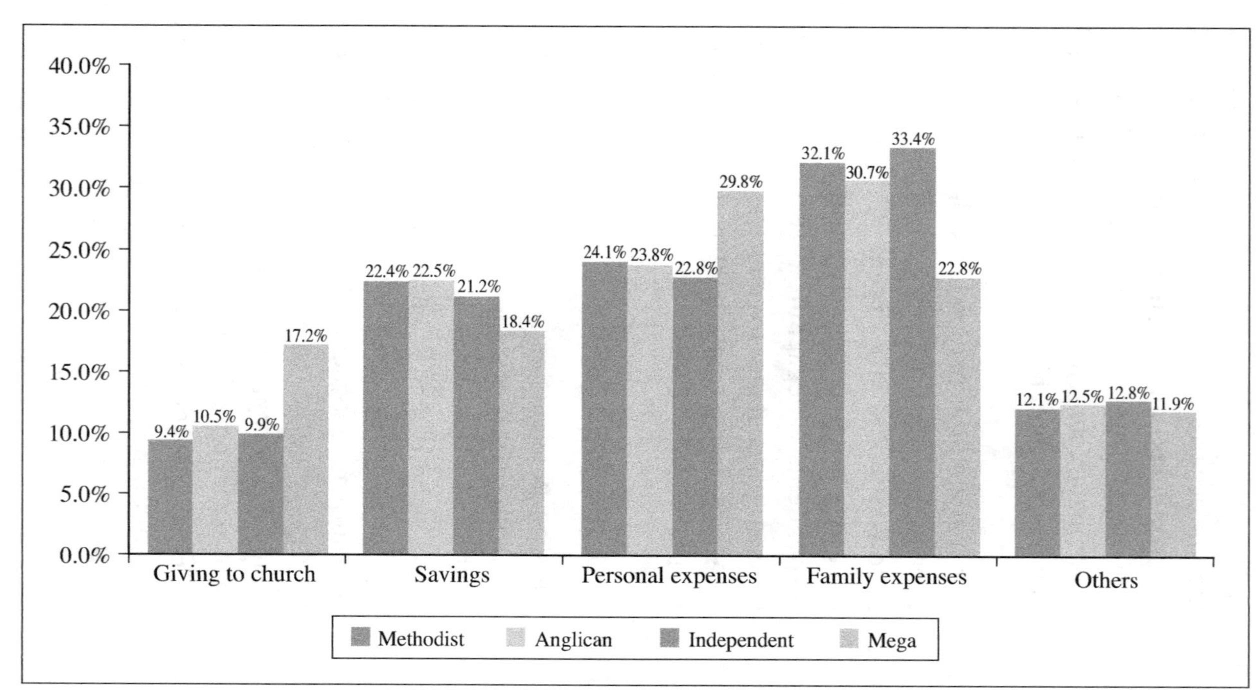

importance to money, while mainline respondents like Methodists and Anglicans tend to have middle class backgrounds.

121. C2.3 *Giving to my church is a form of duty*

Methodist and Anglican respondents were most likely to "agree" or "strongly agree" at 74.5 and 74.4 per cent, respectively. Independents came in at 59.6 per cent and megachurch respondents at 43.0 per cent. We believe that the reason for the discrepancy in response between mainline and megachurch respondents lay in the understanding of the term "duty". Mainline respondents were more likely to have a positive interpretation of the term, that is, giving to church was taken for granted and one's responsibility, hence the higher levels of agreement among the Methodists and Anglicans. Meanwhile megachurch respondents were more likely to interpret the term negatively, that is, giving to church was a chore or compulsion, hence their lower levels of agreement to the statement. Post-survey focus group interviews confirmed our observation.

122. C2.4 *By giving to my church I can expect God to bless me spiritually*

The highest proportion of respondents who answered "agree" or "strongly agree" were megachurch respondents at 75.4 per cent. They were followed by Anglicans at 38.7 per cent; and

Methodists and Independents, both at 35.8 per cent (see Figure C2.4).

123. C2.5 *By giving to my church I can expect God to bless me materially*

The highest proportion of respondents who answered "agree" or "strongly agree" were megachurch respondents at 67.0 per cent. They were followed by Independents at 19.4 per cent; Anglicans at 18.5 per cent; and Methodists at 17.0 per cent (see Figure C2.5). They are consistent with notions of "positive confession" where believers,

Figure C2.4
Expectation of Spiritual Blessing Upon Giving to Church According to Denomination

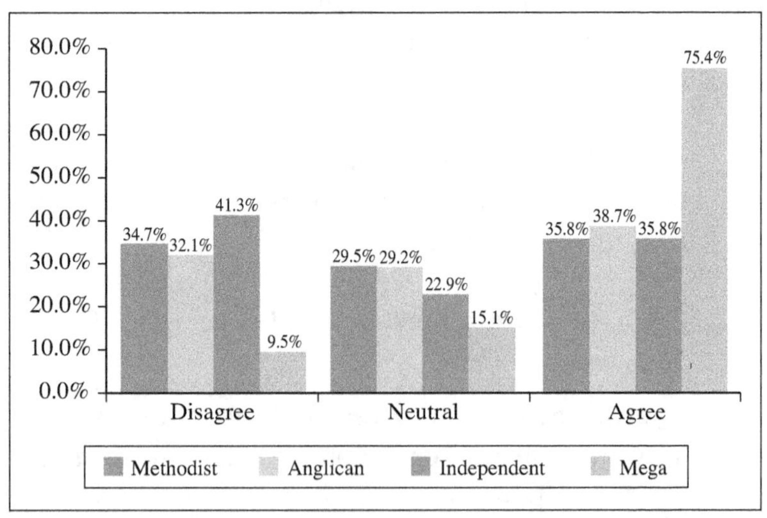

The relation between the variables is significant, X^2 (8, N = 2639) = 394.746, p = .000.

Figure C2.5
Expectation of Material Blessing Upon Giving to Church According to Denomination

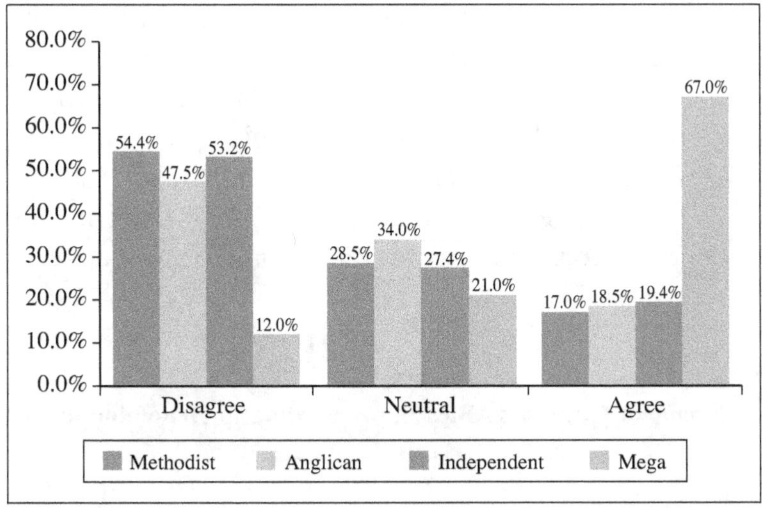

The relation between the variables is significant, X^2 (8, N = 2651) = 702.415, p = .000.

especially Pentecostal Christians, lay claim to God's provisions and promises in the present (Hollinger 1991).

124. C2.9 *The financial growth of my church is a sign of God's blessing over it*

The highest proportion of respondents who answered "agree" or "strongly agree" were megachurch respondents at 71.7 per cent. They were followed by Anglicans at 46.2 per cent; Methodists at 42.0 per cent; and Independents at 40.0 per cent (see Figure C2.9-1). The findings also show that respondents with higher education were less likely to agree with the statement (see Figure C2.9-2). The high percentage of megachurch respondents who responded positively to the statement is in keeping with the broader literature which points to the intimate relationship between megachurches and market logic (see Twitchell 2004; Thumma and Travis 2007). The findings here suggest that market-based key performance indicators which favour quantifiable criteria

Figure C2.9-1
Financial Growth as Blessing According to Denomination

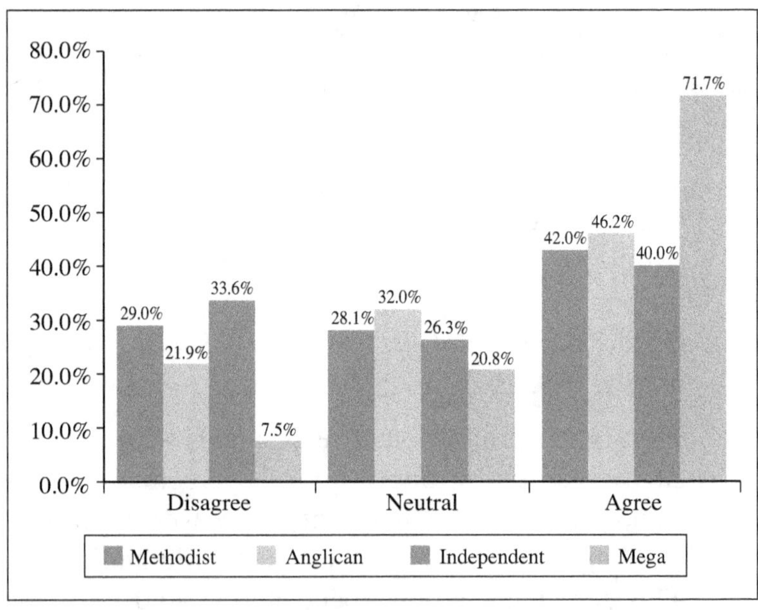

The relation between the variables is significant, X^2 (8, N = 2654) = 270.518, p = .000.

Figure C2.9-2
Financial Growth as Blessing According to Education

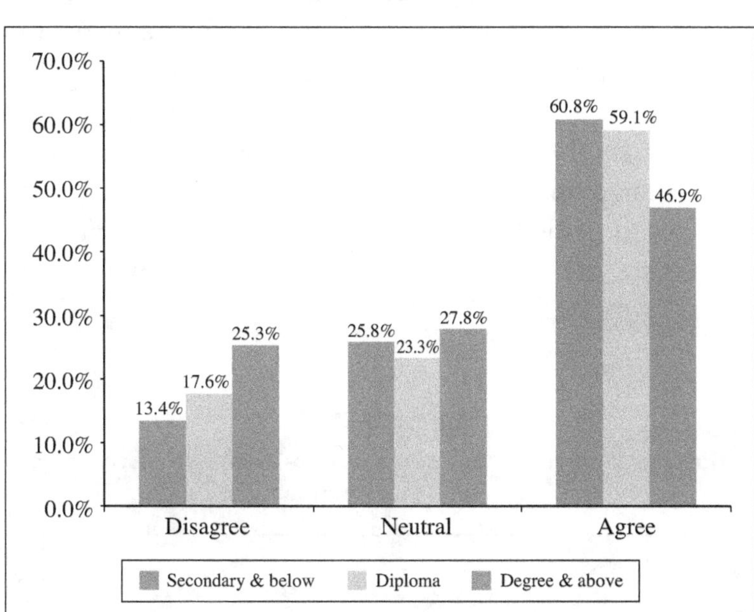

The relation between the variables is significant, X^2 (6, N = 2650) = 58.933, p = .000.

such as numerical and financial growth are seen by megachurch respondents as signs of divine blessing.

125. C2.10 *All full-time staff (e.g. Pastors, church workers, counsellors etc.) should be paid market-competitive salaries*

The highest proportion of respondents who answered "agree" or "strongly agree" were megachurch respondents at 77.6 per cent. They were followed by Independents at 44.8 per cent; Methodists at 42.3 per cent; and Anglicans at 39.8 per cent (see Figure C2.10-1). Again, these findings support the observation of the intimate relationship between megachurches and market strategies, extending market logic to the remuneration of church staff. The findings also show that respondents with diploma and university and above education were more likely to agree with the statement (see Figure C2.10-2).

Figure C2.10-1
Market-Competitive Salaries for Full-Time Staff According to Denomination

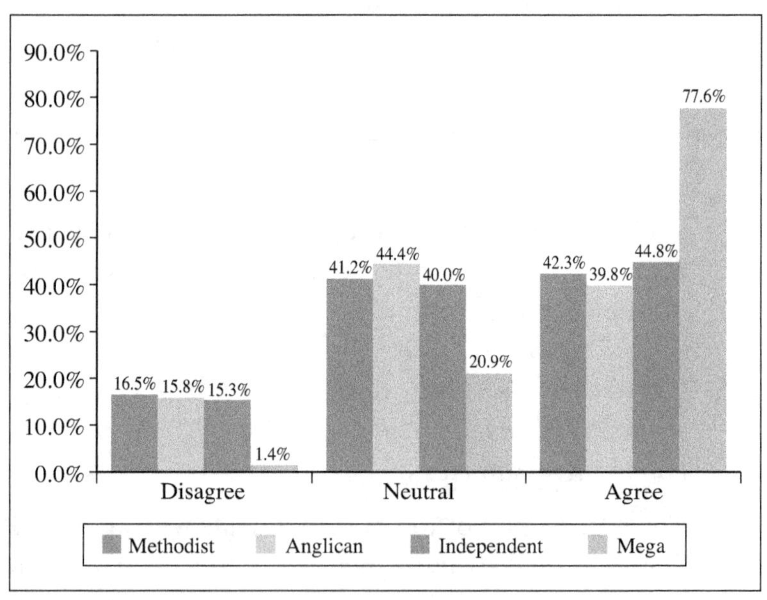

The relation between the variables is significant, X^2 (8, N = 2658) = 361.870, p = .000.

Figure C2.10-2
Market-Competitive Salaries for Full-Time Staff According to Education

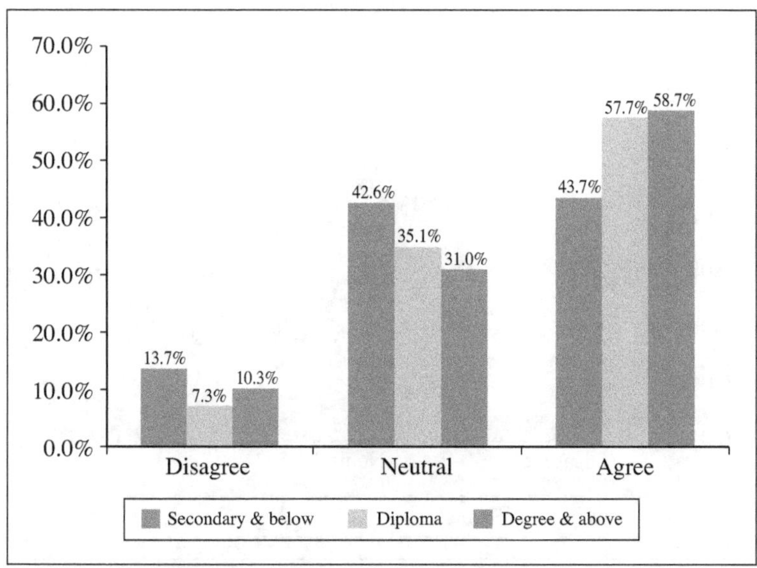

The relation between the variables is significant, X^2 (6, N = 2654) = 54.365, p = .000.

126. C2.11 *The salaries of pastors and church leaders should be in keeping with the size of their congregation or flock*

The highest proportion of respondents who answered "agree" or "strongly agree" were megachurch respondents at 53.8 per cent. This was followed by Methodists at 27.6 per cent; Independents at 27.2 per cent; and Anglicans at 23.5 per cent (see Figure C2.11). Once again, the higher percentage of megachurch respondents who agreed

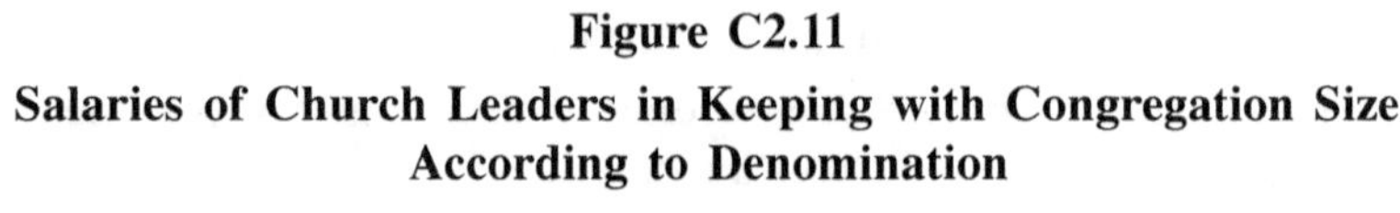

Figure C2.11
Salaries of Church Leaders in Keeping with Congregation Size According to Denomination

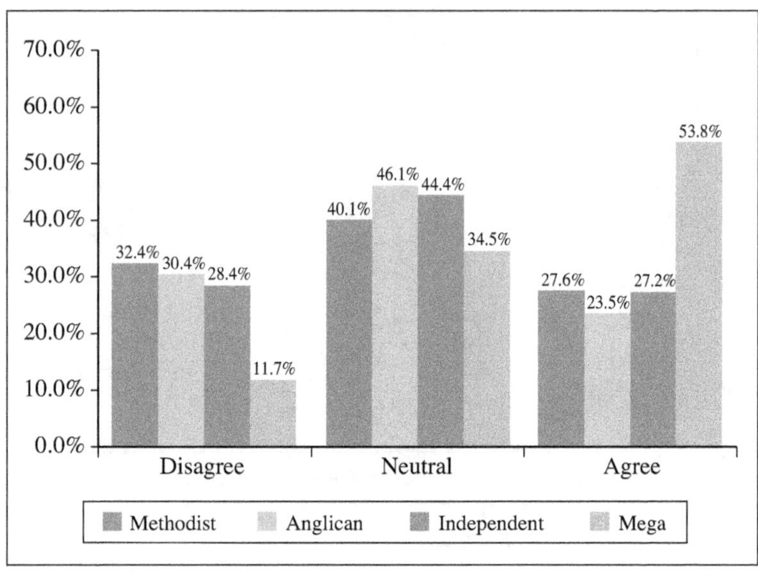

The relation between the variables is significant, X^2 (8, N = 2652) = 253.210, p = .000.

with the statement buttresses the relationship between the megachurch and market logic.

127. C2.12 *I trust my church to deal with its finances honestly*

Megachurch respondents were most likely to "agree" or "strongly agree" at 98.6 per cent. They were followed by Independents at 95.7 per cent; Methodists at 94.3 per cent; and finally Anglicans at 93.1 per cent.

128. C2.14 *If I am a faithful Christian, God will bless me with prosperity*

Megachurch respondents were most likely to "agree" or "strongly agree" at 85.0 per cent. They were followed by Anglicans at 40.8 per cent; Methodists at 39.0 per cent; and Independents at 36.9 per cent (see Figure C2.14-1). Again, these findings support the prevalence of positive confession amongst megachurch respondents. In terms of education, respondents with diplomas and below were more likely to agree with the statement (see Figure C2.14-2).

Figure C2.14-1
Faithful Christians will be Blessed with Prosperity, According to Denomination

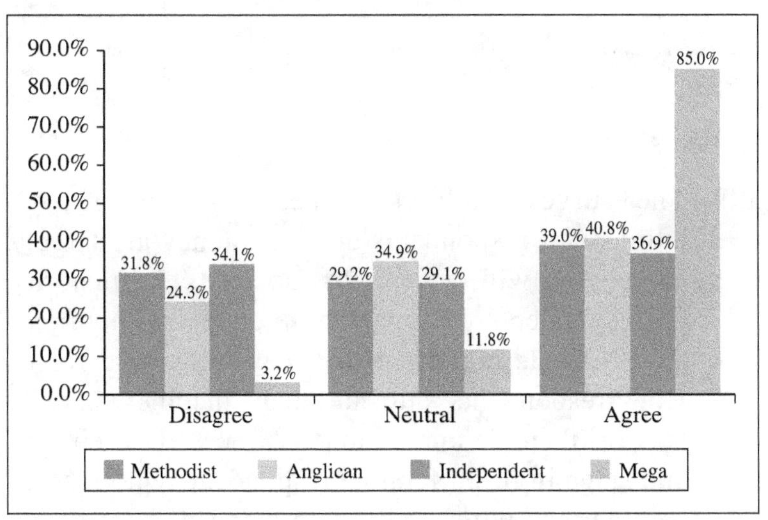

The relation between the variables is significant, X^2 (8, N = 2652) = 576.208, p = .000.

Figure C2.14-2
Faithful Christians will be Blessed with Prosperity, According to Education

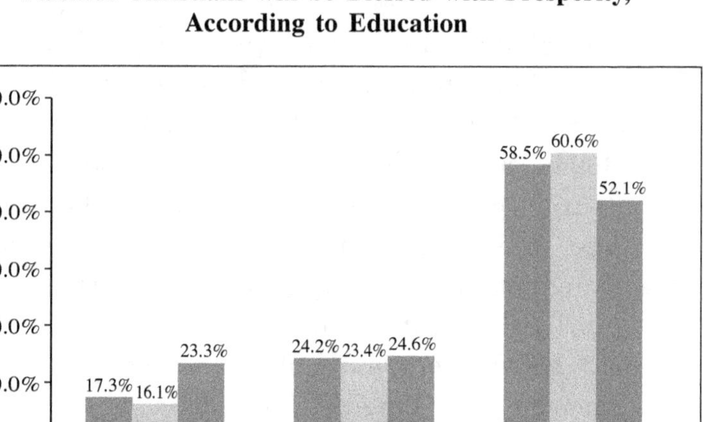

The relation between the variables is significant, X^2 (6, N = 2648) = 25.660, p = .000.

Conclusion

129. The survey findings suggest that the general attitudes of respondents towards money are largely in keeping with a capitalist society. The majority of respondents believe that money is important, and that it is important that they work hard for it. How respondents allocate their income depends less on their denomination but more on their age and stage in life. Mainline respondents who tend to be older and with families are more likely to spend more of their income on "family expenses" while megachurch respondents, who tend to be younger with fewer family commitments, spend more on "personal expenses".

130. There seems to be a general pattern according to denomination when it comes to the nexus between attitudes towards money and spirituality. Mainline respondents are more likely to maintain a separation of money matters and market logic from church life and notions of faithfulness. In other words, money or material abundance is less likely to be seen as outward indicators of God's blessings or a person's faithfulness. Set in the broader context, mainline respondents display what Bruce (2002, p. 19; see also Bruce 2010) terms the "compartmentalization and privatization" of religion. Here, it is argued, the increased secularization of society leads to the compartmentalization of faith in order to facilitate greater social negotiation which, in turn, results in the privatization of faith whereby "the reach of religion is shortened to just those who accept the teachings of this or that faith" (Bruce 2002, p. 20). In short, the distinction between church and secular life, spiritual and material, private and public, believer and non-believer is made with greater clarity.

131. Conversely, two observations with regards to megachurch respondents may be made. Firstly, in contrast to mainline respondents, megachurch respondents were less likely to display the compartmentalization and privatization of faith. Instead, the latter were more likely to demonstrate a stronger nexus between money matters or market logic and church life or faithfulness. The findings suggest that these respondents are more open to the application of market logic and practices (such as market competitive salaries and salaries pegged to congregation size) to church administrative and organizational practices. In this context, megachurches in Singapore seem to buttress the broader literature which observes that American megachurches incorporate marketing practices in organizational and recruitment strategies (Twitchell 2004; Thumma and Travis 2007).

132. Secondly, this survey suggests that megachurch respondents are more likely to have a positive view of the relationship between money and faithfulness where money or wealth may be an indicator of God's blessing or a person's faithfulness. However, it is unclear as to whether the inverse is true, namely, that megachurch respondents see the *lack* of money or wealth as signs of a person's *lack* of faithfulness or *absence* of God's blessings. These findings support the assertion that the "gospel of prosperity" has become increasingly global through "charismatic Christianity", especially "in large urban areas with middle-class constituencies" (Coleman 2000, p. 27). The prosperity gospels should not be narrowly defined as the quest for material or financial gain but, rather, as the broader desire to claim the "good life" as promised by God in the here and now. According to Coleman (1993, p. 355) the prosperity gospels are the blending of "Pentecostal revivalism with elements of positive thinking" and the belief that God desires followers to enjoy life to the fullest extent, including financial prosperity, good health and the fulfilling of individual potential, and are often accompanied by notions of "positive confession" where believers lay claim to God's provisions and promises in the present.

133. This is particularly interesting because scholars are divided over whether the prosperity gospels appeal to the poor because it offers hope for upward mobility (Cox 2001) or to the wealthy because it serves as divine legitimacy of their social status (Bruce 1990). At neither end of the extreme, the findings here suggest that the ethos of the Singapore megachurch shares "elective affinity" (Weber 1991) with the aspirations of young upwardly mobile Singaporeans. The megachurch in Singapore is a site that expresses Christianity in the language of market practice and logic, thus converging with and appealing to the economic aspirations and consumer habits of many young upwardly mobile Singaporeans. These young Singaporeans, in turn, not only find a brand of spirituality that is privileged in capitalist Singapore, but also familiarity with other Singaporeans of similar backgrounds undergoing the same class transitions as they are.

Section E: Politics

134. This section considers attitudes towards politics, especially the degree to which Christian values and Christians should intervene in the public life of Singapore. As Mathews (2009) has argued, Christians in Singapore have, in recent years, articulated a "voice of conscience" on issues and public policies that are at odds with Christian values. To gauge the influence of religious values on political outlook, respondents were asked to respond to 5-point Likert items associated with statements that link their religious values with politics.

135. E1.1 *The religion of a political candidate or government leader is important to me.*

Fifty-four per cent of Methodists, 50.1 per cent of Anglicans, 48.1 per cent of Independents and 46.6 per cent of megachurch respondents either agree or strongly agree with this statement. The difference between the various denominations is marginal (see Figure E1.1).

136. E2.1 *My Christian values influence my views on public policy issues (e.g. casinos, abortion).*

Eighty-six per cent of Methodists, 83.6 per cent of Anglicans, 87.2 per cent of Independents and 87.9 per cent of megachurch respondents agree or strongly agree with this statement. In general, Christian values very much influence views on

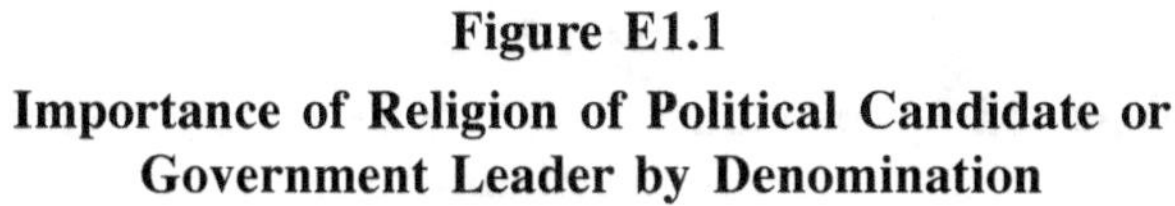

Figure E1.1
Importance of Religion of Political Candidate or Government Leader by Denomination

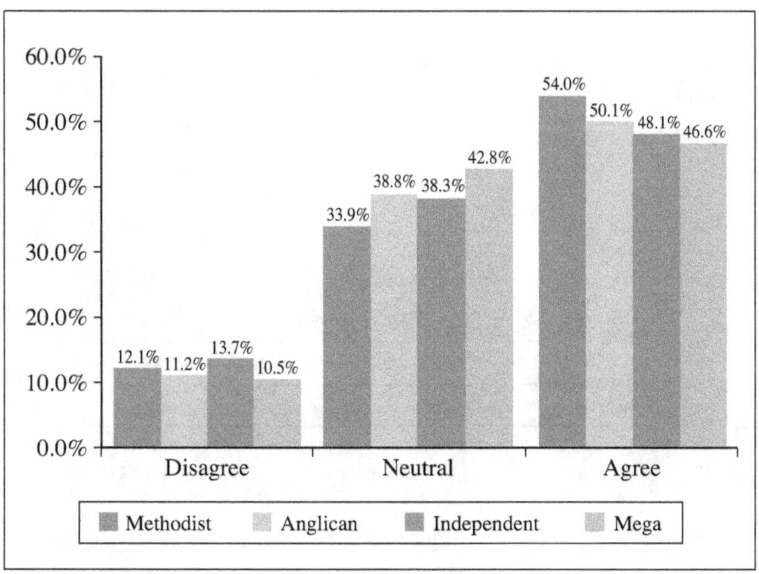

The relation between the variables is significant, X^2 (8, N = 2661) = 15.580, p = .049.

public policy but there is no clear distinction across denominations (see Figure E2.1-1).

However, when we cross-tabulate responses with educational level, the more educated respondents are marginally more likely to agree or strongly agree with the statement. Thus, 80.6 per cent of those with secondary education and below, 83.4 per cent of those with diplomas and 90.3 per cent of those with university degrees and above agree or strongly agree with the statement (see Figure E2.1-2).

Figure E2.1-1

Influence of Christian Values on Views on Public Policy Issues by Denomination

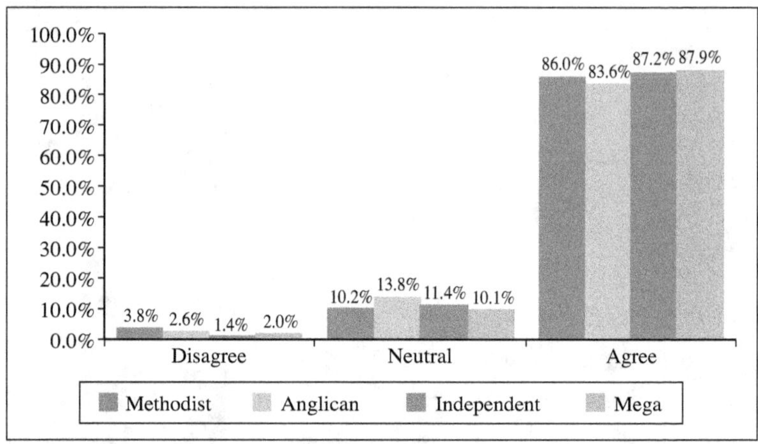

The relation between the variables is insignificant, X^2 (8, N = 2663) = 13.968, p = .083.

Figure E2.1-2

Influence of Christian Values on Views on Public Policy Issues by Educational Level

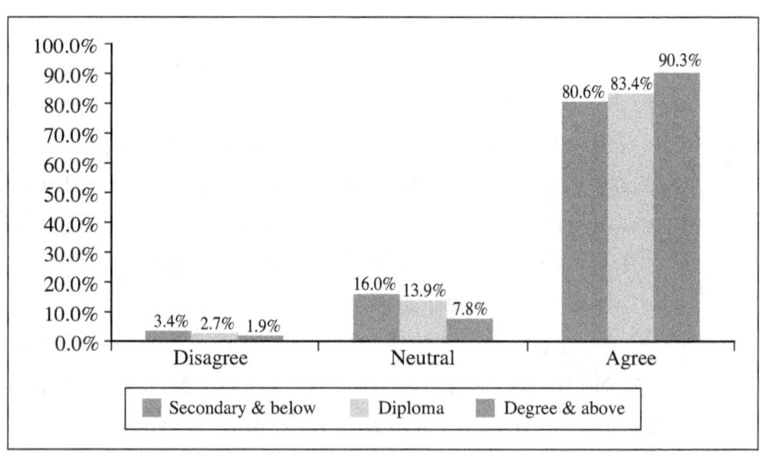

The relation between the variables is significant, X^2 (6, N = 2659) = 42.903, p = .000.

137. E2.3 *Christians should collectively express their views on public policy issues in public.*

Fifty-six point seven per cent of Methodists, 52.1 per cent of Anglicans, 49.2 per cent of Independents and 33.3 per cent of megachurch respondents agree or strongly agree with this statement. Here, megachurch respondents appear to be less keen on intervening in the public sphere as a religious collective (see Figure E2.3).

Figure E2.3
Expression of Views on Public Policy Issues in Public by Denomination

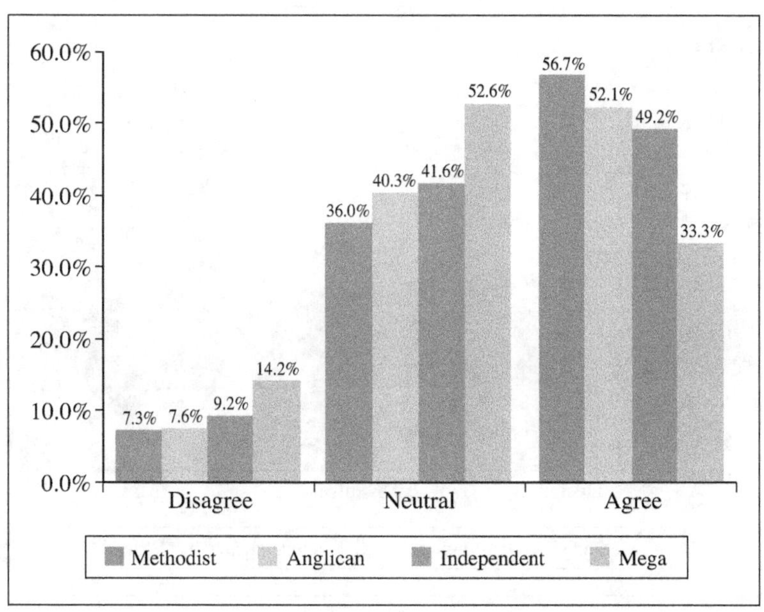

The relation between the variables is significant, X^2 (8, N = 2656) = 106.443, p = .000.

138. E2.4 *It is acceptable to support Christians active in causes or issues that are not church-related (e.g. casinos, abortion).*

Fifty-one point seven per cent of Methodists, 46.0 per cent of Anglicans, 46.5 per cent of Independents and 45.1 per cent of megachurch respondents agree or strongly agree with this statement. The distinction between the different denominations is slight (see Figure E2.4-1).

Figure E2.4-1

Supporting Christians Active in Causes or Issues that are not Church-related by Denomination

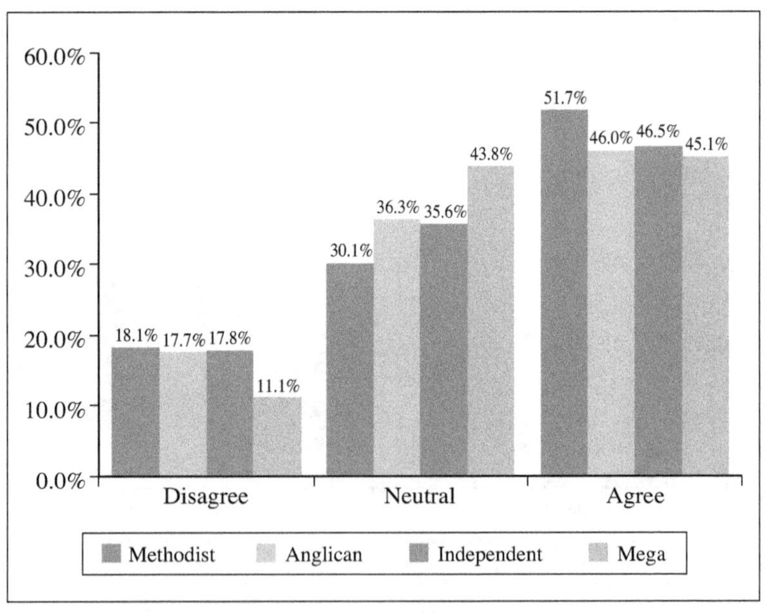

The relation between the variables is significant, X^2 (8, N = 2646) = 43.480, p = .000.

When we cross-tabulate responses with educational level, the more educated respondents are slightly more likely to agree or strongly agree with the statement. Thus, 39.0 per cent of those with secondary education and below, 42.1 per cent of those with diplomas and 52.8 per cent of those with university degrees and above agree or strongly agree with the statement (see Figure E2.4-2).

Figure E2.4-2

Supporting Christians Active in Causes or Issues that are not Church-related by Educational Level

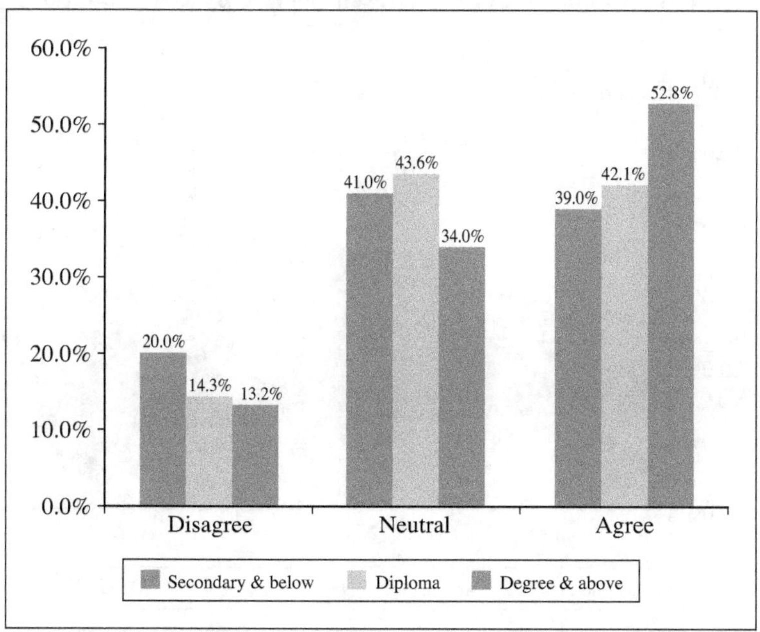

The relation between the variables is significant, X^2 (6, N = 2642) = 49.565, p = .000.

139. E2.5 *It is acceptable for my pastor to comment on civil society or public policy matters over the pulpit or during church service.*

Fifty point two per cent of Methodists, 40.9 per cent of Anglicans, 39.0 per cent of Independents and 36.1 per cent of megachurch respondents agree or strongly agree with this statement. It appears that Methodists are slightly more likely to agree with this statement (see Figure E2.5).

Figure E2.5

Pastor Commenting on Civil Society or Public Policy Matters over the Pulpit or during Church Service by Denomination

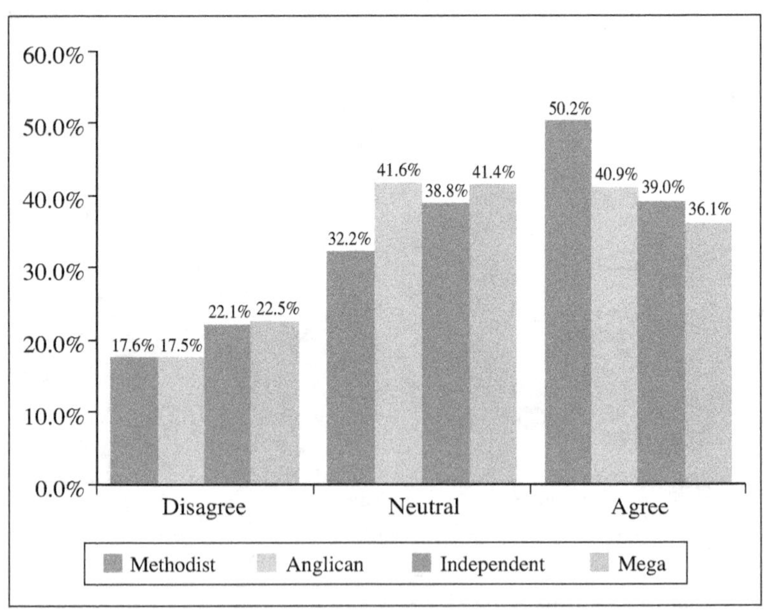

The relation between the variables is significant, X^2 (8, N = 2654) = 36.727, p = .000.

140. E3.1 *The Singapore government is becoming too liberal in terms of moral values.*

Forty-six per cent of Methodists, 42.7 per cent of Anglicans, 45.2 per cent of Independents and 28.0 per cent of megachurch respondents agree or strongly agree with this statement. As such, megachurch respondents are less likely to agree with this statement in comparison with respondents from mainline and independent churches (see Figure E3.1).

Figure E3.1

Opinions on Singapore Government Becoming Too Liberal in terms of Moral Values by Denomination

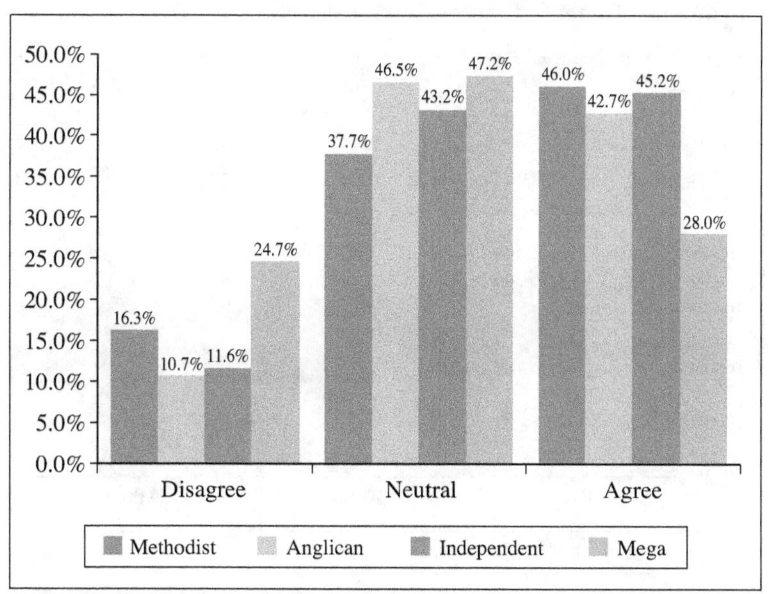

The relation between the variables is significant, X^2 (8, N = 2658) = 108.132, p = .000.

141. E3.2 *When it comes to public policies, the Singapore government is more concerned with economic benefits than with moral values.*

Sixty point three per cent of Methodists, 62.2 per cent of Anglicans, 60.3 per cent of Independents and 40.8 per cent of megachurch respondents agree or strongly agree with this statement. It is evident that megachurch respondents are less likely to agree with this statement in comparison with respondents from mainline and independent churches (see Figure E3.2).

Figure E3.2

Opinions on Singapore Government More Concerned with Economic Benefits than with Moral Values by Denomination

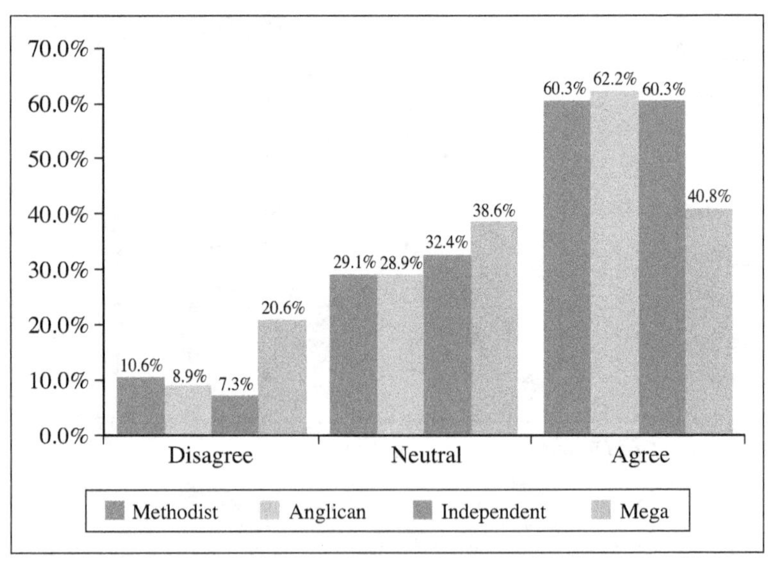

The relation between the variables is significant, X^2 (8, N = 2658) = 125.944, p = .000.

Conclusion

142. While megachurch respondents are as likely as respondents from mainline and independent churches to allow their Christian values to influence their views on public policies, they are less likely to view the moral character of public policy in Singapore with concern, and are also less likely to support intervening in public policy matters through the public sphere.

143. During follow-up focus group sessions with respondents from megachurches, morality was articulated as a private matter. As such, moral influence is to be exercised through one's private capacity in spheres that one is active in, rather than by imposing values through the church as a civic organization. In being disinclined towards exercising moral influence through the public sphere, it appears that megachurch respondents tend towards a compartmentalization of their religious and political lives. However, this does not imply that these respondents do not seek to exert moral influence in society; it is just that the channels employed are spiritual empowerment and corporate strategies rather than conventional civil society (Goh 2010).

144. Concerning some of these statements, we also find that the level of education has a significant influence. While across denominations, Christians seek a fit between their Christian values and views on public policy, those with higher education have a higher propensity to do so. At the same time, those with higher education are also more likely to support civil society causes undertaken by Christians.

Section G: Sex and Sexuality

145. This section explores the relationship between Christian values and sex and sexuality through 5-point Likert items. Some of the issues explored include pre-marital sex, homosexuality, abortion and sex education. With regards to homosexuality, a distinction is made between attitude and practice through asking "yes/no" questions to gauge the level of interaction with homosexuals.

146. G1.1 *Pre-marital sex (sex before marriage) is fine as long as those involved are consenting adults and if they practise safe sex.*

Eighty-one point five per cent of Methodists, 81.1 per cent of Anglicans, 84.9 per cent of Independents and 93.1 per cent of megachurch respondents disagree or strongly disagree with this statement. As such, megachurch respondents are slightly more likely to disagree with this statement in comparison with respondents from mainline and independent churches (see Figure G1.1).

Figure G1.1
Opinions on Pre-Marital Sex by Denomination

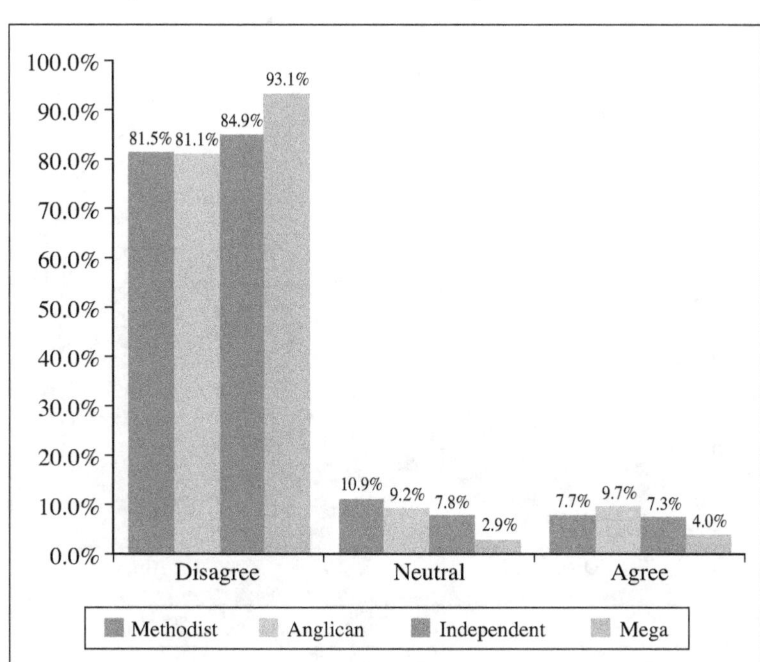

The relation between the variables is significant, X^2 (8, N = 2657) = 76.601, p = .000.

147. G1.3 *It is morally wrong to engage in homosexuality (same sex sexual relations).*

Eighty-two point three per cent of Methodists, 79.7 per cent of Anglicans, 81.5 per cent of Independents and 85.7 per cent of megachurch respondents agree or strongly agree with this statement. The distinction between denominations is quite marginal (see Figure G1.3-1).

Figure G1.3-1
Opinions on Morality of Homosexuality by Denomination

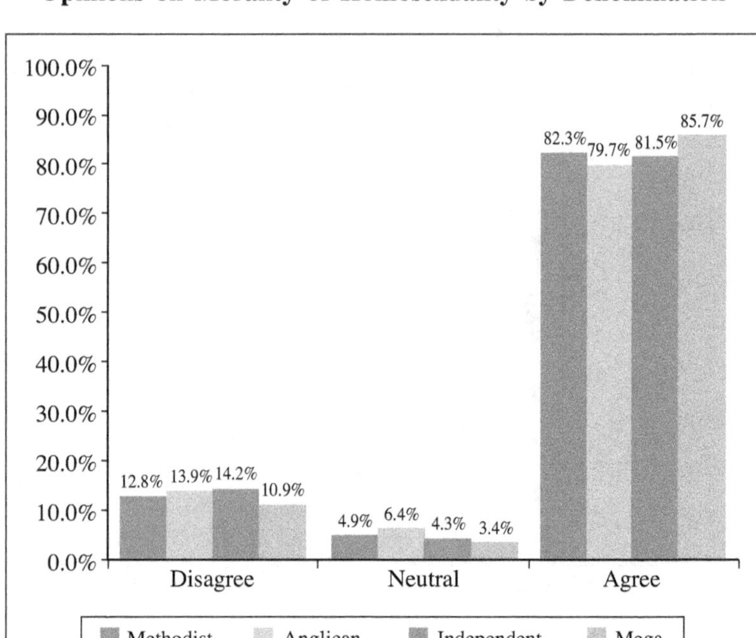

The relation between the variables is significant, X^2 (8, N = 2653) = 15.935, p = .043.

When we cross-tabulate responses with educational level, the more educated respondents are marginally more likely to agree or strongly agree with the statement. Thus, 78.8 per cent of those with secondary education and below, 81.5 per cent of those with diplomas and 85.5 per cent of those with university degrees and above agree or strongly agree with the statement (see Figure G1.3-2).

Figure G1.3-2
Opinions on Morality of Homosexuality by Educational Level

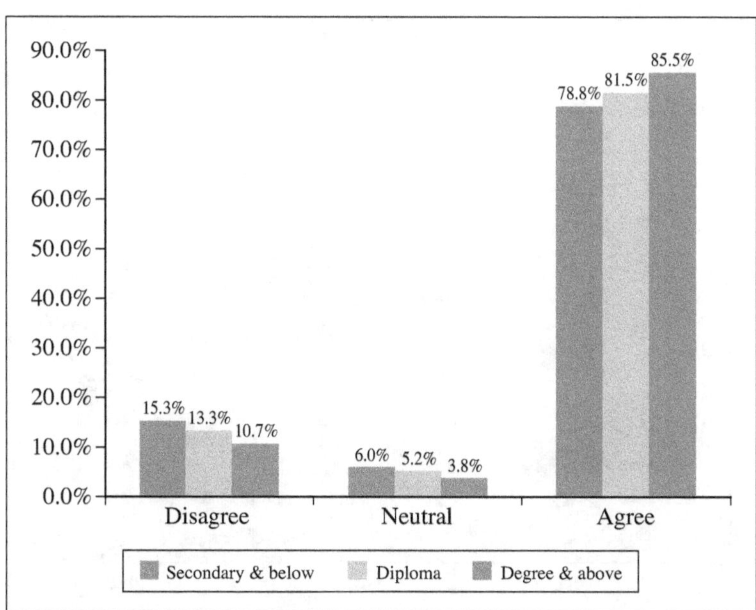

The relation between the variables is significant, X^2 (6, N = 2649) = 16.633, p = .011.

148. G1.4 *I feel comfortable interacting with homosexuals.*

Thirty-seven point nine per cent of Methodists, 32.2 per cent of Anglicans, 28.0 per cent of Independents and 59.2 per cent of megachurch respondents agree or strongly agree with this statement. Megachurch respondents are much more likely to agree with this statement in comparison with respondents from mainline and independent churches (see Figure G1.4-1).

Figure G1.4-1

Comfortable Interacting with Homosexuals by Denomination

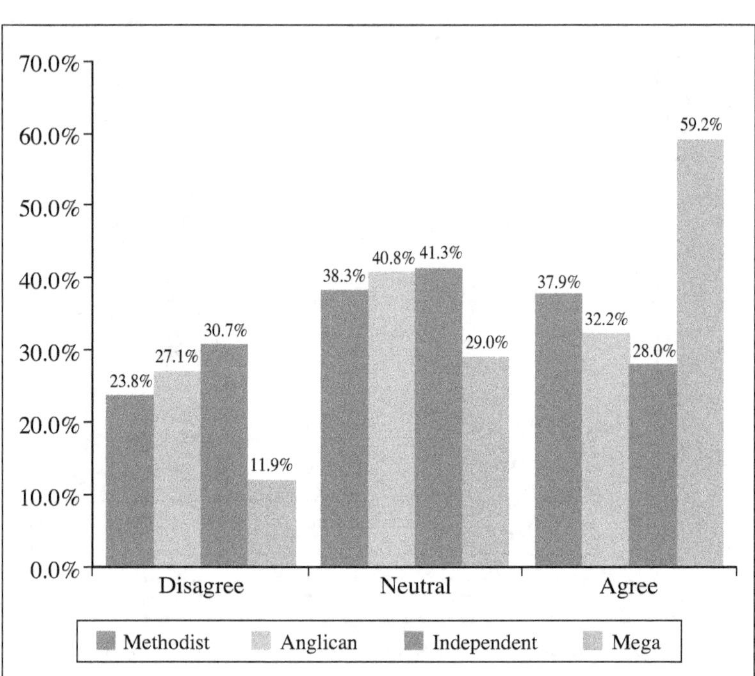

The relation between the variables is significant, X^2 (8, N = 2650) = 196.352, p = .000.

When we cross-tabulate responses with educational level, the more educated respondents are more likely to agree or strongly agree with the statement. Thus, 33.0 per cent of those with secondary education and below, 38.4 per cent of those with diplomas and 49.2 per cent of those with university degrees and above agree or strongly agree with the statement (see Figure G1.4-2).

Figure G1.4-2
Comfortable Interacting with Homosexuals by Educational Level

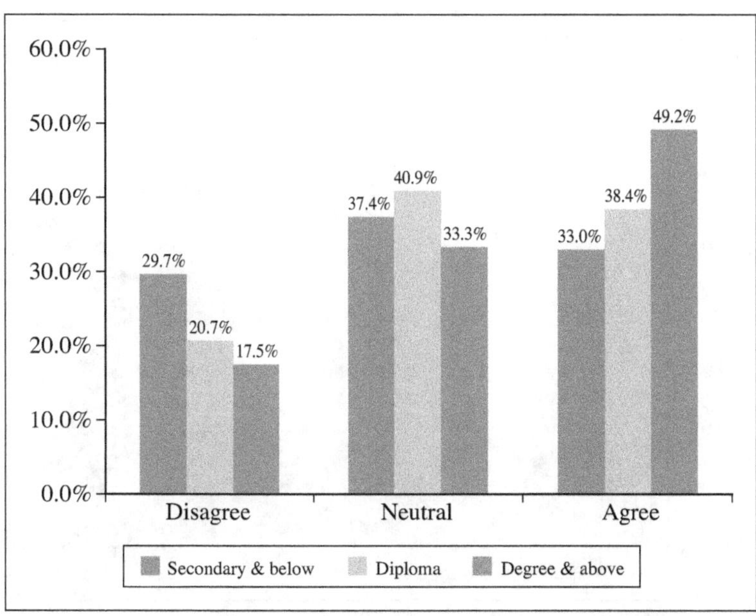

The relation between the variables is significant, X^2 (6, N = 2646) = 73.710, p = .000.

149. G1.5 *I do not mind making friends with homosexuals.*

Fifty-four point eight per cent of Methodists, 46.7 per cent of Anglicans, 46.3 per cent of Independents and 75.2 per cent of megachurch respondents agree or strongly agree with this statement. Thus, it appears that megachurch respondents are much more likely to agree with this statement in comparison with respondents from mainline and independent churches (see Figure G1.5).

Figure G1.5
Making Friends with Homosexuals by Denomination

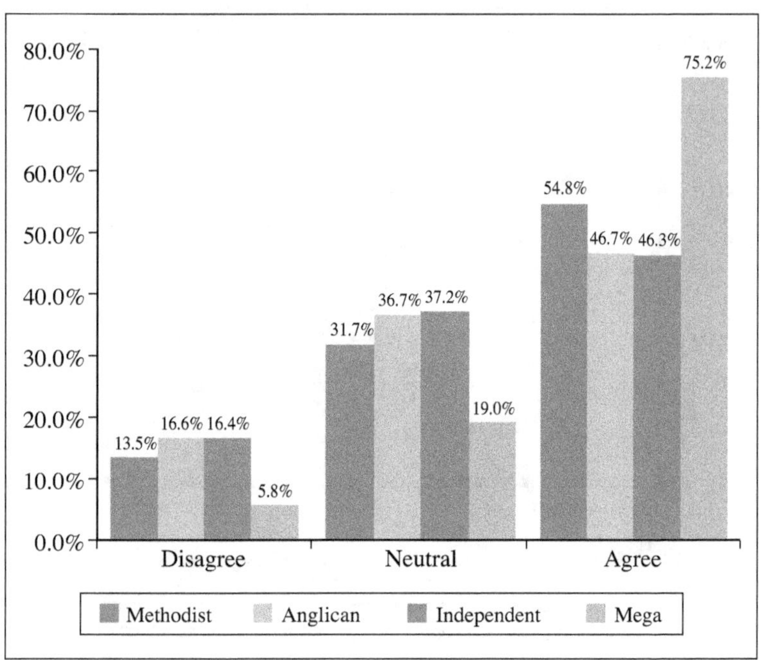

The relation between the variables is significant, X^2 (8, N = 2656) = 184.509, p = .000.

150. G1.6 *I do not mind a homosexual family member.*

Fourteen per cent of Methodists, 11.4 per cent of Anglicans, 8.9 per cent of Independents and 26.5 per cent of megachurch respondents agree or strongly agree with this statement. As such, megachurch respondents are more likely to agree with this statement in comparison with respondents from mainline and independent churches (see Figure G1.6).

Figure G1.6
Not Minding a Homosexual Family Member by Denomination

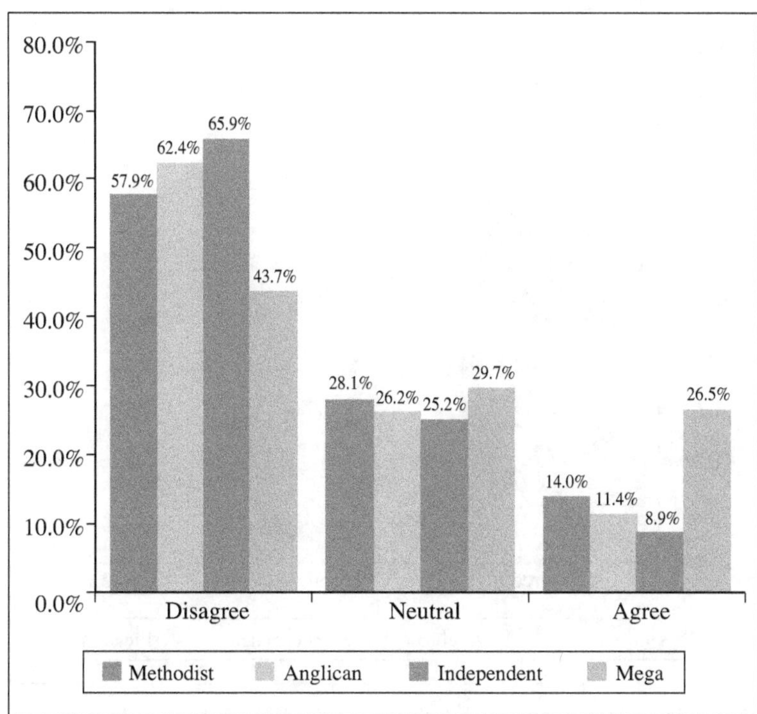

The relation between the variables is significant, X^2 (8, N = 2645) = 132.994, p = .000.

151. G1.7 *I do not mind a homosexual church leader.*

Eighty-four point nine per cent of Methodists, 84.7 per cent of Anglicans, 88.6 per cent of Independents and 86.2 per cent of megachurch respondents disagree or strongly disagree with this statement. The distinction across denominations is marginal (see Figure G1.7).

Figure G1.7
Not Minding a Homosexual Church Leader by Denomination

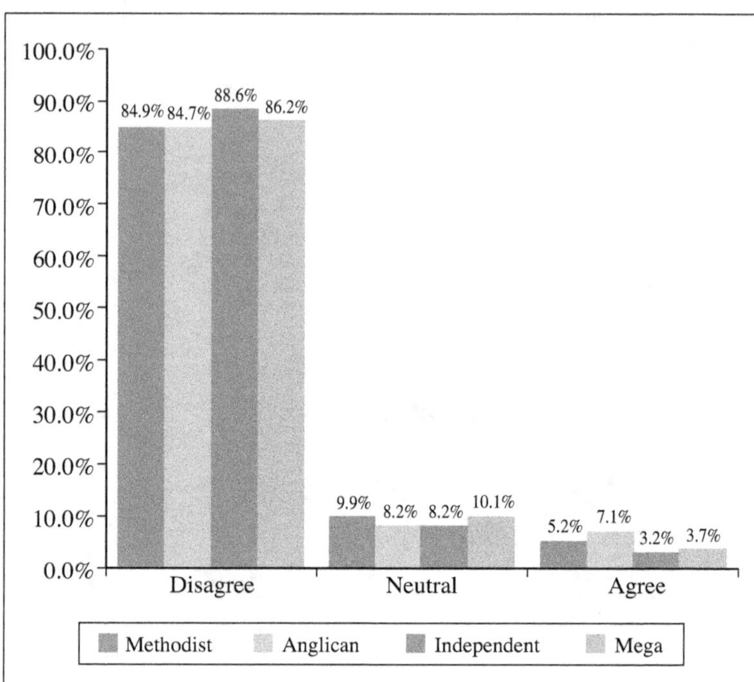

The relation between the variables is significant, X^2 (8, N = 2653) = 16.343, p = .038.

152. G2.1 *Do you have friends who are homosexuals?*

Forty-three point one per cent of Methodists, 39.7 per cent of Anglicans, 43.1 per cent of Independents and 62.9 per cent of megachurch respondents answered "yes" to this question. Thus, megachurch respondents are more likely than respondents from mainline and independent churches to have friends who are homosexuals (see Figure G2.1-1).

Figure G2.1-1
Homosexual Friends by Denomination

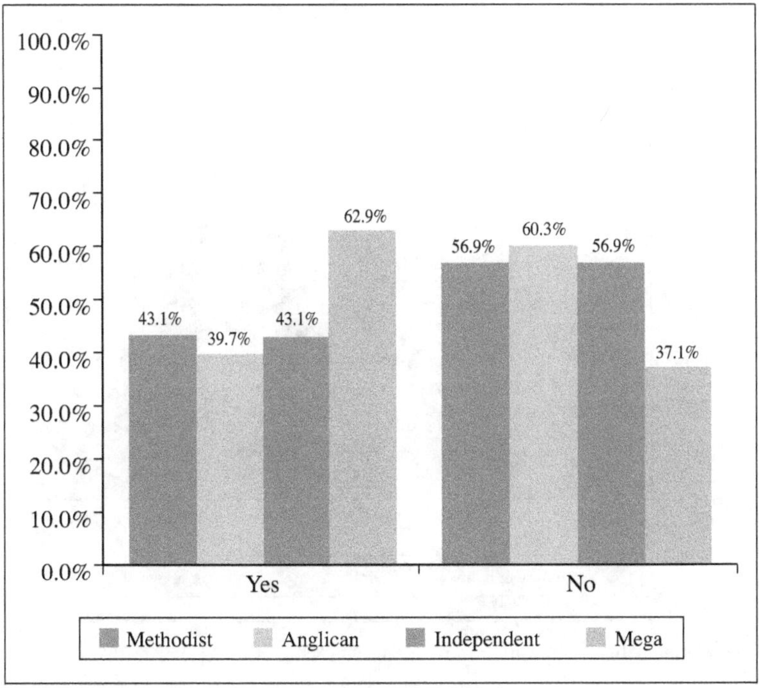

	Methodist	Anglican	Independent	Mega
Yes	43.1%	39.7%	43.1%	62.9%
No	56.9%	60.3%	56.9%	37.1%

The relation between the variables is significant, X^2 (4, N = 2624) = 113.577, p = .000.

When we cross-tabulate responses with educational level, the more educated respondents are more likely to have friends who are homosexuals. Thus, 37.9 per cent of those with secondary education and below, 48.2 per cent of those with diplomas and 55.6 per cent of those with university degrees and above answered "yes" to the question (see Figure G2.1-2).

Figure G2.1-2
Homosexual Friends by Educational Level

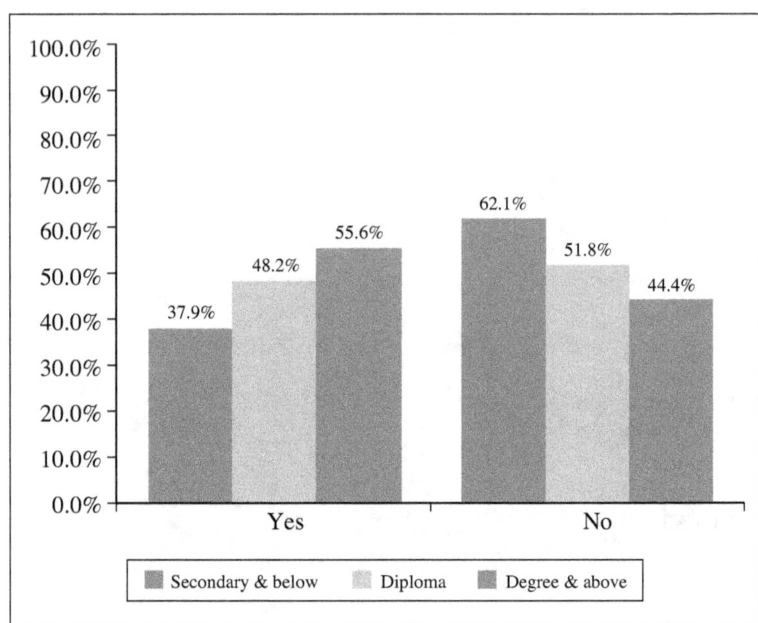

The relation between the variables is significant, X^2 (3, N = 2621) = 55.761, p = .000.

153. G2.2 *Do you go out with friends who are homosexuals?*

Thirty-one point three per cent of Methodists, 32.2 per cent of Anglicans, 31.0 per cent of Independents and 56.2 per cent of megachurch respondents answered "yes" to this question. Thus, megachurch respondents are more likely than respondents from mainline and independent churches to go out with friends who are homosexuals (see Figure G2.2-1).

Figure G2.2-1
Going Out with Homosexual Friends by Denomination

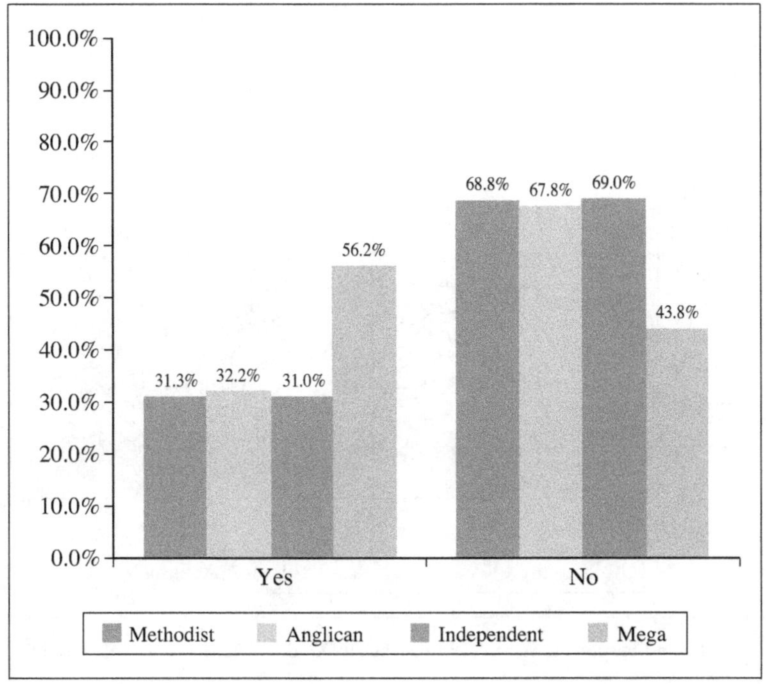

The relation between the variables is significant, X^2 (4, N = 2598) = 162.991, p = .000.

When we cross-tabulate responses with educational level, the more educated respondents are more likely to go out with friends who are homosexuals. Thus, 30.9 per cent of those with secondary education and below, 41.7 per cent of those with diplomas and 44.3 per cent of those with university degrees and above answered "yes" to the question (see Figure G2.2-2).

Figure G2.2-2
Going Out with Homosexual Friends by Educational Level

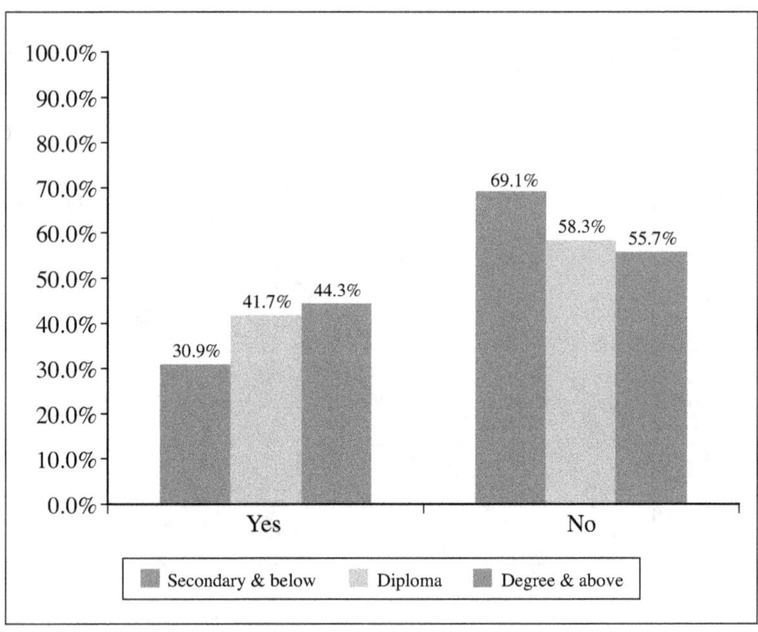

The relation between the variables is significant, X^2 (3, N = 2595) = 33.942, p = .000.

154. G2.3 *Do you have family members who are homosexuals?*

Five point six per cent of Methodists, 4.0 per cent of Anglicans, 3.3 per cent of Independents and 4.0 per cent of megachurch respondents answered "yes" to this question. Thus, affirmative answers to this question are low across all denominations (see Figure G2.3). The difference is statistically insignificant across denominations.

Figure G2.3
Having Homosexual Family Members by Denomination

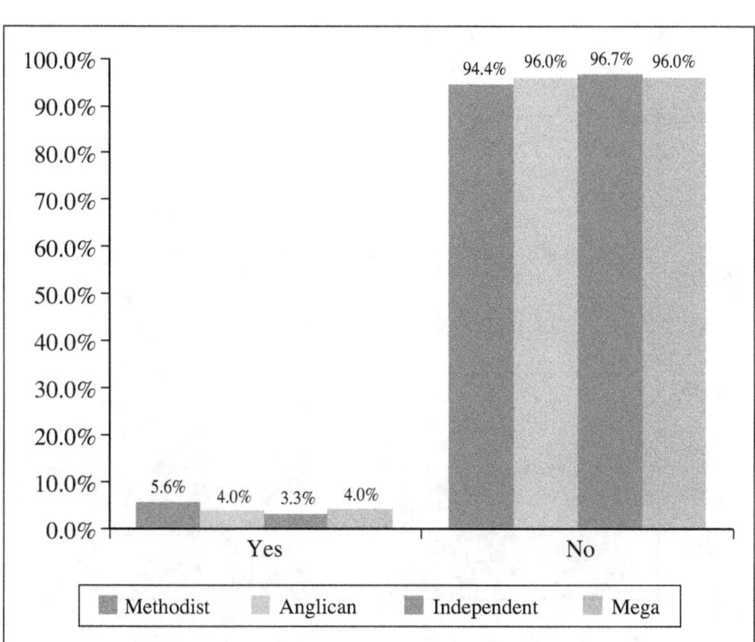

The relation between the variables is insignificant, X^2 (4, N = 2625) = 5.07961, p = .279.

155. G2.4 *Do you know Christians who are homosexuals?*

Twenty-six per cent of Methodists, 20.5 per cent of Anglicans, 22.5 per cent of Independents and 35.6 per cent of megachurch respondents answered "yes" to this question. Thus, megachurch respondents are more likely to know Christians who are homosexuals, as compared with respondents from mainline and independent churches (see Figure G2.4).

Figure G2.4
Knowing Homosexual Christians by Denomination

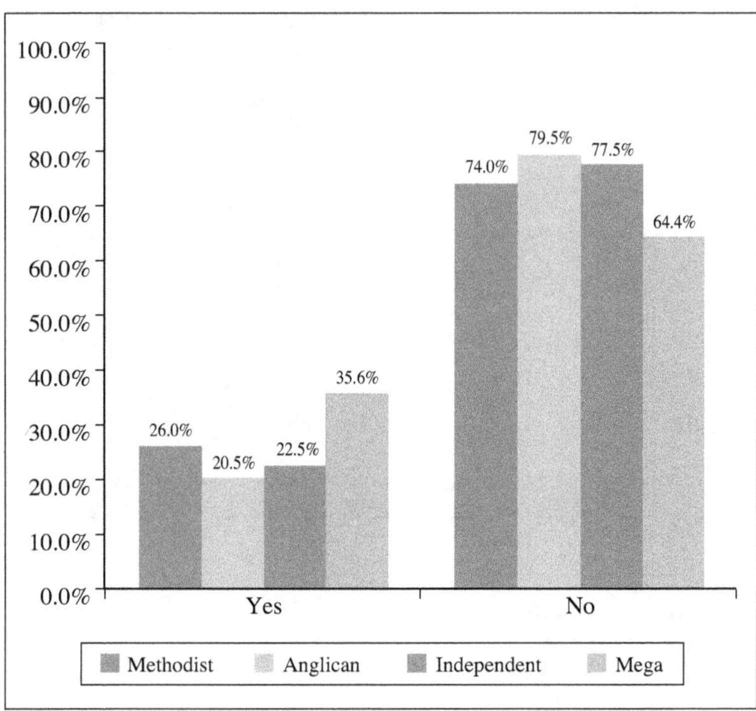

The relation between the variables is significant, X^2 (4, N = 2613) = 59.910, p = .000.

156. G3.1 *Abortion is morally wrong.*

Seventy-six point seven per cent of Methodists, 78.8 per cent of Anglicans, 77.1 per cent of Independents and 92.9 per cent of megachurch respondents agree or strongly agree with the statement. It appears that megachurch respondents are more likely to agree with the statement (see Figure G3.1).

Figure G3.1
Opinion on Morality of Abortion by Denomination

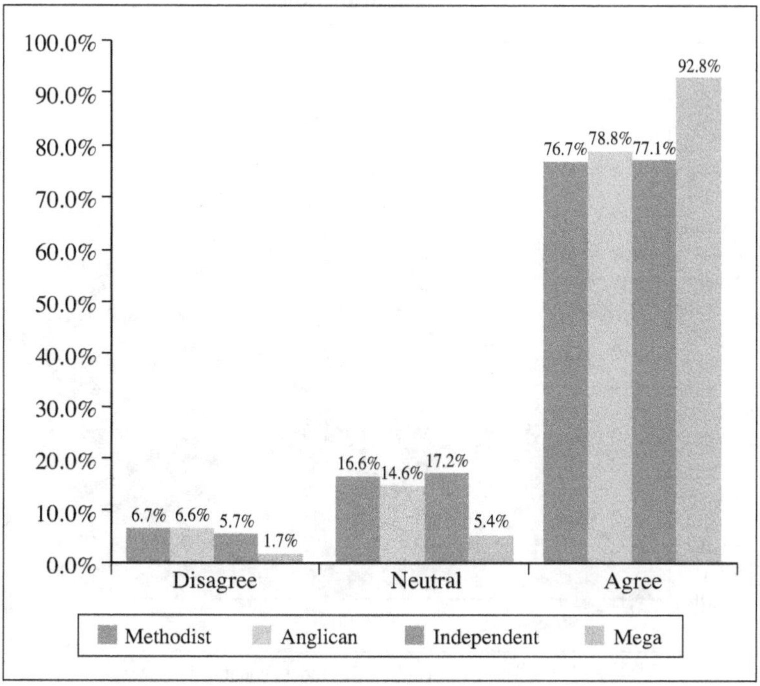

The relation between the variables is significant, X^2 (8, N = 2659) = 114.377, p = .000.

157. G3.2 *Abortion should be made illegal in Singapore.*

Forty point six per cent of Methodists, 44.3 per cent of Anglicans, 38.9 per cent of Independents and 37.7 per cent of megachurch respondents agree or strongly agree with the statement. Although megachurch respondents appear to be least likely to agree with the statement, the distinction across denominations is marginal (see Figure G3.2).

Figure G3.2
Opinion on whether Abortion should be made Illegal by Denomination

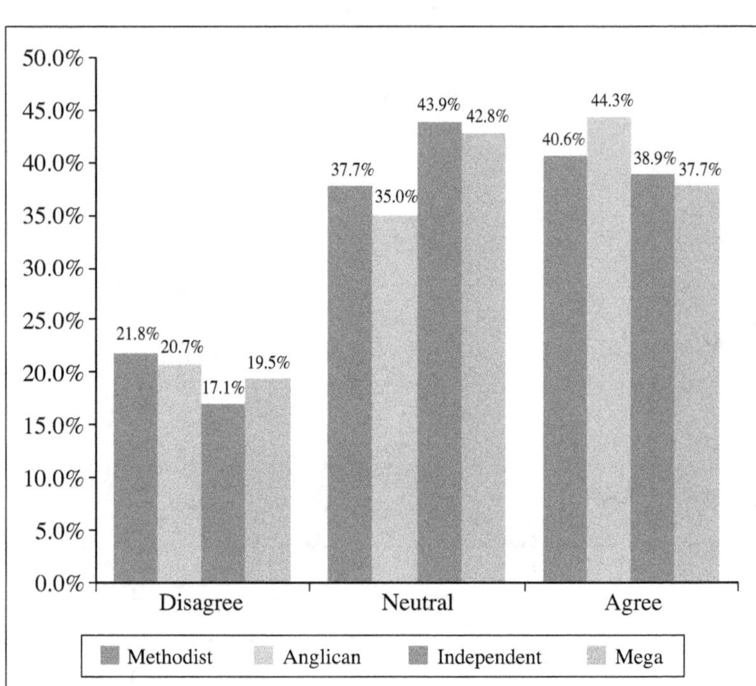

The relation between the variables is significant, X^2 (8, N = 2658) = 18.655, p = .017.

158. G5.1 *Sex education in Singapore schools today is too liberal.*

Twenty-eight point eight per cent of Methodists, 26.9 per cent of Anglicans, 30.3 per cent of Independents and 19.1 per cent of megachurch respondents agree or strongly agree with the statement. On the other hand, 20.4 per cent of

Methodists, 18.3 per cent of Anglicans, 21.8 per cent of Independents and 28.7 per cent of megachurch respondents disagree or strongly disagree with the statement. As such, megachurch respondents are less likely to agree with the statement and more likely to disagree with the statement, as compared with respondents from mainline and independent churches (see Figure G5.1).

Figure G5.1
Opinion on Sex Education being Too Liberal in Singapore by Denomination

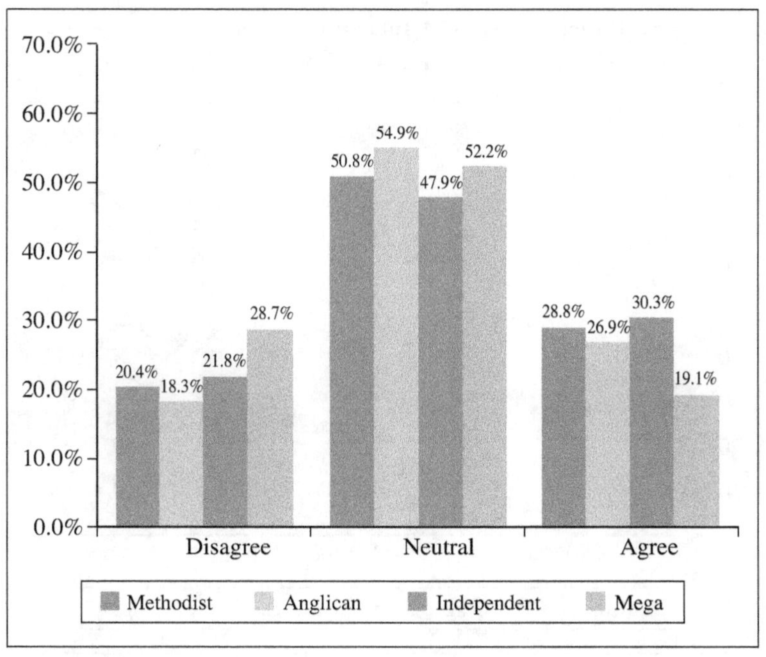

The relation between the variables is significant, X^2 (8, N = 2651) = 48.864, p = .000.

159. G.5.2 *Sex education should incorporate more moral or religious values.*

Eighty-one point two per cent of Methodists, 78.3 per cent of Anglicans, 76.7 per cent of Independents and 69.2 per cent of megachurch respondents agree or strongly agree with the statement. Thus, megachurch respondents are slightly less likely to agree with the statement, as compared with respondents from mainline and independent churches (see Figure G5.2).

Figure G5.2
Sex Education should Incorporate more Moral or Religious Values by Denomination

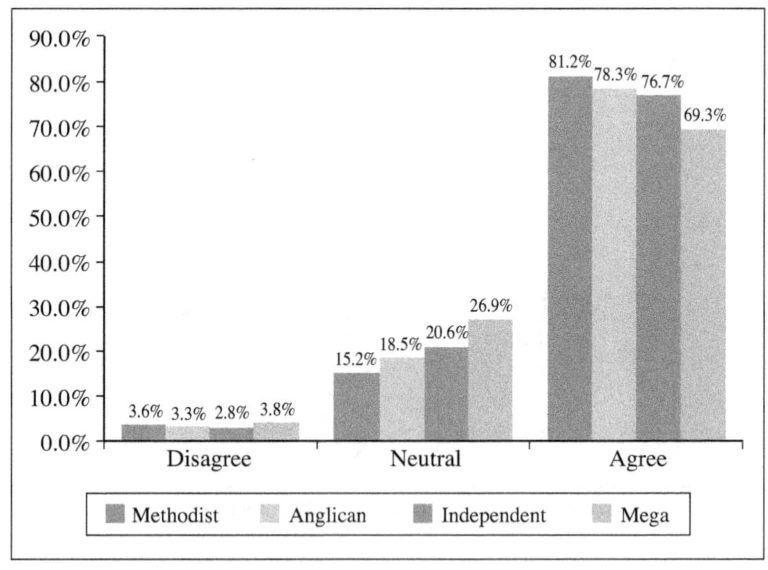

The relation between the variables is significant, X^2 (8, N = 2658) = 36.498, p = .000.

Conclusion

160. In general, we find that megachurch respondents are as conservative, if not more conservative, in comparison with respondents from mainline and independent churches with regard to values related to sex and sexuality. This is the case concerning pre-marital sex, the moral status of homosexuality and abortion.

161. Concerning attitudes towards homosexuals, megachurch respondents are more willing to interact with and have friends who are homosexuals. In terms of practice, megachurch respondents are also more likely to have friends who are homosexuals and go out with them. The more homosexual-friendly stance of megachurch respondents probably has to do with the "seeker church" orientation of megachurches, whereby the distance between the church and the outside world is minimized to demonstrate the relevance of Christianity (Sargeant 2000; Thumma and Travis 2007). In the conscious attempt to situate the church in close proximity with the marketplace (Tong 2008, p. 199), it is possible that megachurch respondents find themselves in closer proximity with a broader cross-section of Singapore's middle-class. However, the greater acceptance and level of interaction with regard to homosexuals do not imply moral approval of homosexuality, as a strong majority disagree with the institution of homosexual church leaders.

162. In our post-survey focus group discussion with respondents from megachurches, we find that a high premium is placed on the acceptance of people as they are. While homosexuality is considered morally wrong, it is not singled out as being more morally deplorable. That is, respondents refrain from attaching a stigma to homosexuals and from being judgmental in their interactions with homosexuals. At the same time, leaders are expected to conform to certain values of the church, and as such should not be practising homosexuality.

163. Our findings also show that while the better educated are more likely to consider homosexuality morally wrong, they are also more accepting of homosexuals and more likely to have homosexual friends and go out with them. This may be because homosexuals are more likely to be found in the social networks of the better educated.

164. While megachurch respondents are morally conservative, they are less inclined to want to apply their moral yardstick in the public sphere, as compared with respondents from mainline and independent churches. Megachurch respondents are less inclined to agree with making abortion illegal, although they more strongly agree that abortion is morally wrong. They are also less inclined to judge sex education in Singapore as being too liberal, and less inclined to support the incorporation of moral or religious values into sex education. This pattern accords with the compartmentalization discussed in the last section, whereby megachurch respondents are reluctant to let their religious values impinge on the public sphere.

Section H: Other Religions and Communities

165. One of the most challenging issues facing multicultural and multireligious societies today is the balance between faithfulness to one's religious tenets and respect for the religious sensitivities of others. The broader literature has shown that Christians in multicultural societies may experience tensions between their religious and civic identities because of the different demands and responsibilities that come with these different identities (Bramadat and Seljak 2008; Turner 2010).

166. Specifically, for Singapore, one of the key concerns in a multicultural society is the relationship between different faith communities as well as attitudes towards proselytization. This section has three objectives. Firstly, it seeks to survey the respondents' *perception* of other religions and communities; secondly, it gauges the attitudes of respondents towards proselytizing in a multicultural society; and thirdly, it gauges the social habits of respondents with regards to friends from other faiths.

167. H1.1 *Christian values are compatible with those of different ethnic or cultural communities.*[6]

Megachurch respondents are most likely to "agree" with this statement at 51.5 per cent, while independent church respondents are most likely to "disagree" with it at 27.5 per cent (see Figure H1.1). Large percentages of respondents across denominations chose "neutral". This may indicate that they had no opinion on the matter or did not want to register a negative or positive answer.

Figure H1.1

Compatibility of Christian Values with Different Ethnic or Cultural Communities According to Denomination

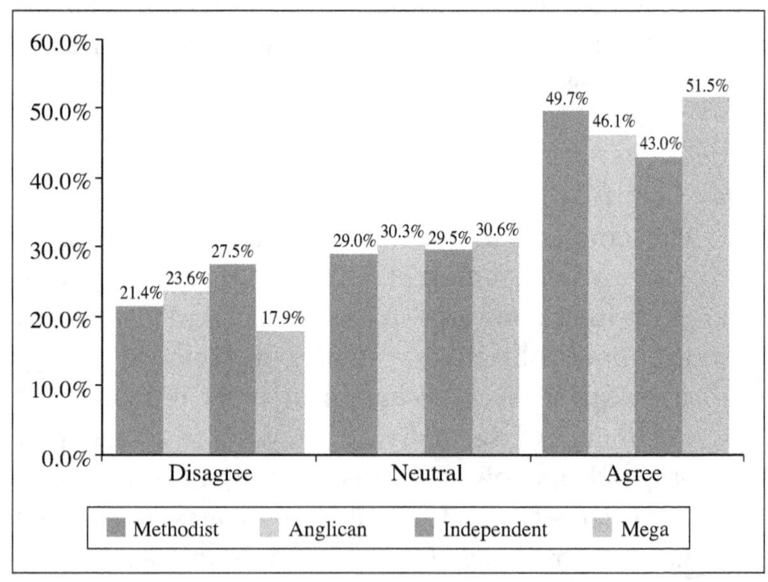

The relation between the variables is significant, X^2 (8, N = 2653) = 25.322, p = .001.

168. H1.2 *Christian values are compatible with those of different religious communities.*

Megachurch respondents are most likely to "agree" with this statement at 45.4 per cent, while independent church respondents are most likely to "disagree" with it at 34.5 per cent (see Figure H1.2). Again, large percentages of respondents across denominations chose "neutral". This may indicate that they had no opinion on the matter or did not wish to register a negative or positive answer.

Figure H1.2
Compatibility of Christian Values with Different Religious Communities According to Denomination

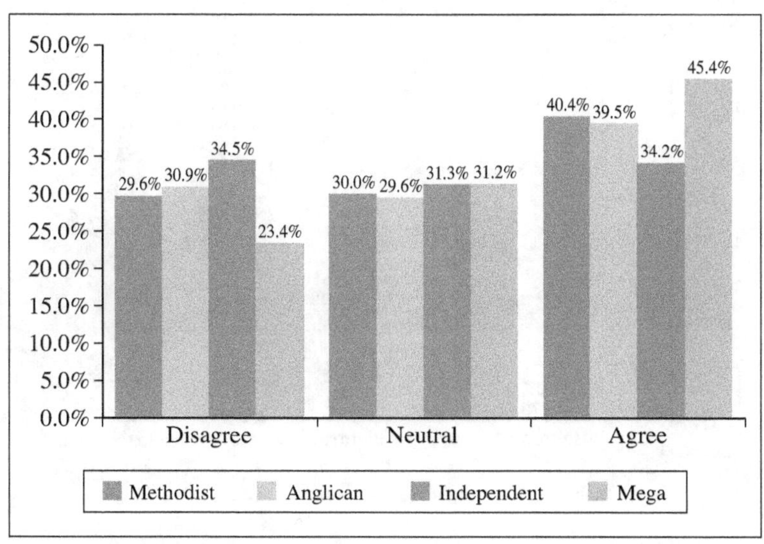

The relation between the variables is significant, X^2 (8, N = 2650) = 34.234, p = .000.

169. H2.4 *I believe that the message of God's Word can overcome ethnic and religious sensitivities in Singapore.*

The majority of respondents across denominations agreed with this statement (see Figure H2.4). The findings were similar across ages and education. This suggests a broad and strong conviction that spreading the Gospel has divine purpose, which is enough to negotiate earthly obstacles such as ethnic and religious sensitivities.

Figure H2.4

Belief that God's Word can Overcome Religious and Ethnic Sensitivities According to Denomination

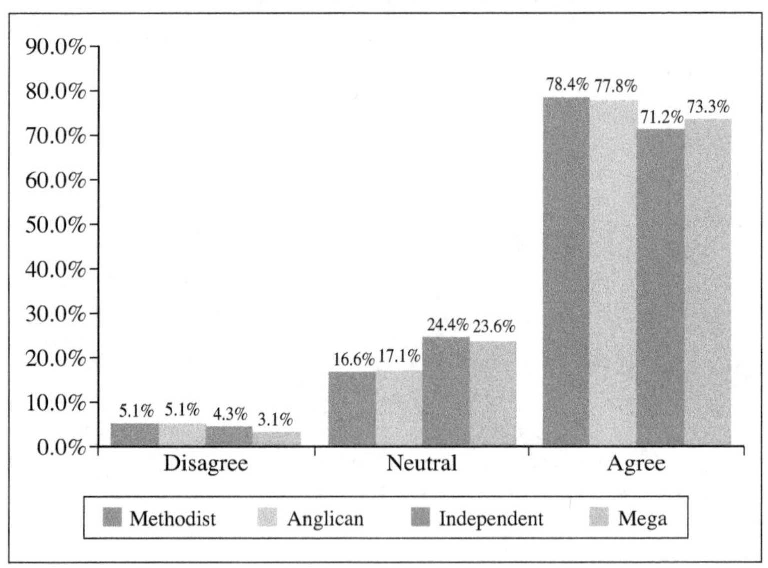

The relation between the variables is significant, X^2 (8, N = 2652) = 24.043, p = .002.

170. H2.5 *People of different religions need to hear the Word of God.*

The majority of respondents across denominations agreed with this statement (see Figure H2.5). The findings were similar across ages and education. Again, this demonstrates the strong and long-term conviction amongst Christians to spread the Gospel, consistent with the overall belief in the Great Commission.[7]

Figure H2.5

Belief that People of Different Religions need to hear God's Word According to Denomination

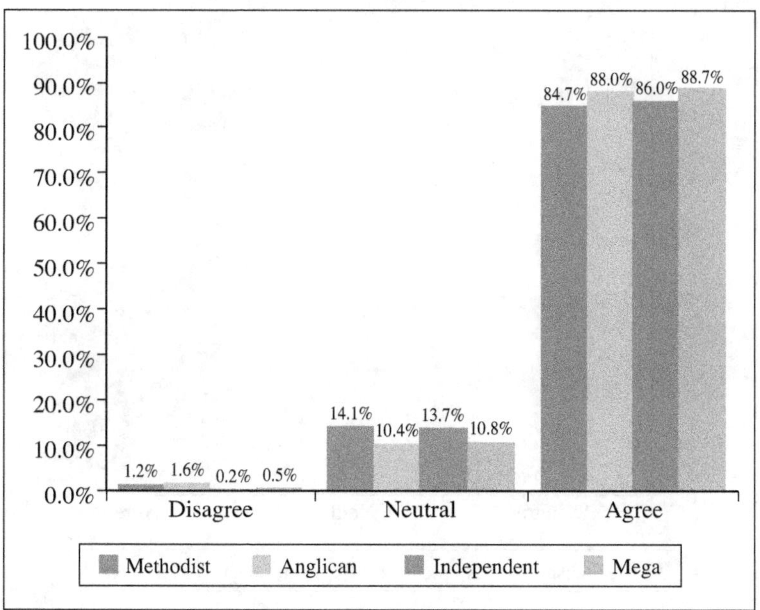

The relation between the variables is insignificant, X^2 (8, N = 2654) = 15.403, p = .052.

171. H2.6 *I believe God has commanded Christians to evangelize to everyone.*

The majority of respondents across denominations agreed with this statement (see Figure H2.6). The findings were similar across ages and education. As above, this confirms the conviction amongst Christians to spread the Gospel.

Figure H2.6
Belief that God has commanded Christians to Evangelize to Everyone According to Denomination

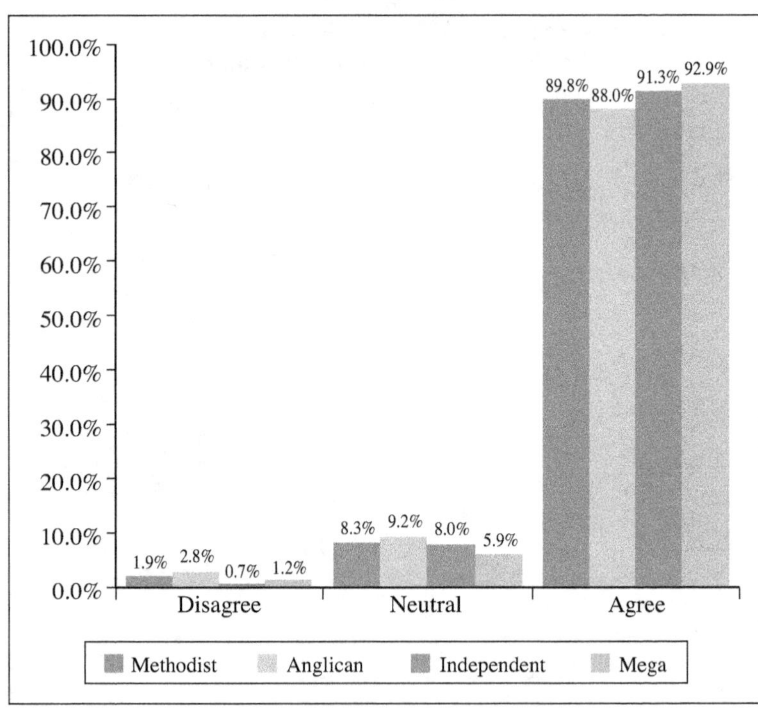

The relation between the variables is significant, X^2 (8, N = 2659) = 17.244, p = .028.

172. H2.7 *Unfriendly reactions from people of other religions are God's test of Christians' perseverance in spreading his Word.*

Megachurch respondents were less likely to "agree", and more likely to "disagree", suggesting that they are more sensitive to negative reactions from those of other religions. This is keeping with the trend that megachurch respondents have greater interaction with Buddhist and Taoist communities, or come from such backgrounds (see Figure H2.7-1). When cross-tabulated with

Figure H2.7-1

Belief that Unfriendly Reactions are God's Test of Christians' Perseverance According to Denomination

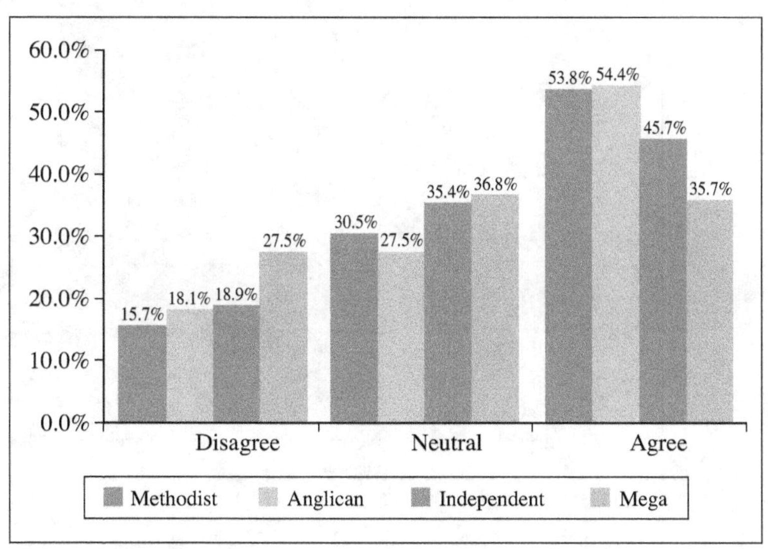

The relation between the variables is significant, X^2 (8, N = 2652) = 82.830, p = .000.

education, it was found that graduate respondents were less likely to agree at 42.2 per cent, compared to respondents with secondary education or lower at 53.6 per cent (see Figure H2.7-2).

Figure H2.7-2

Belief that Unfriendly Reactions are God's Test of Christians' Perseverance According to Education

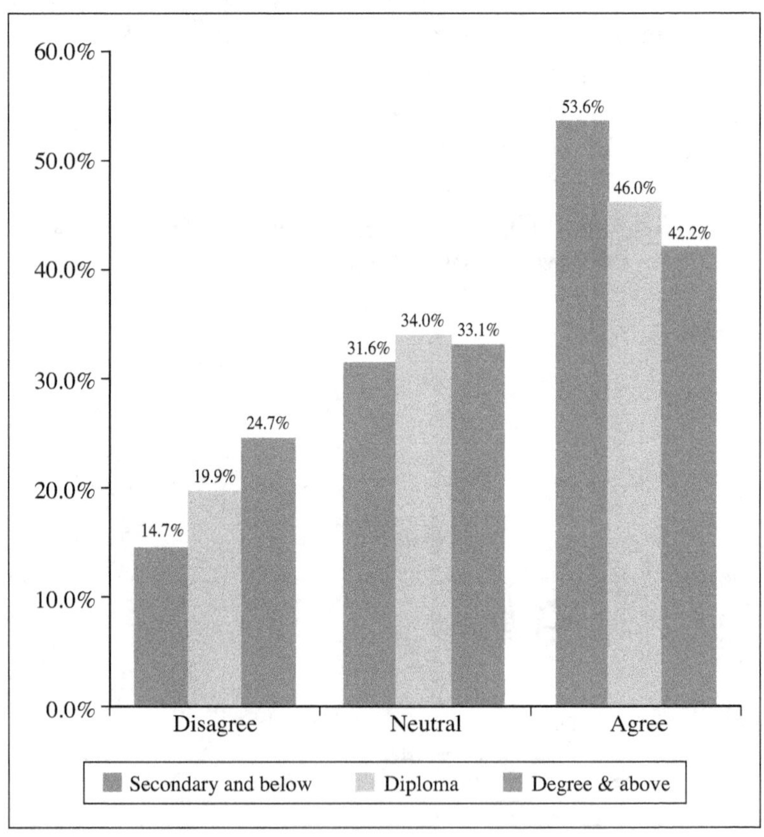

The relation between the variables is significant, X^2 (6, N = 2648) = 37.535, p = .000.

173. H2.8 *Spreading the message that God loves all his children is not offensive to non-religious people or people of other faiths.*

The majority of respondents across denominations agreed with this statement (see Figure H2.8). The findings were similar across ages and education. This suggests that respondents believe that the message of God's love, which is presumably the message of tolerance, affirmation and inclusion, will be viewed positively by those of other faiths.

Figure H2.8

Belief that Spreading the Message of God's Love is Not Offensive According to Denomination

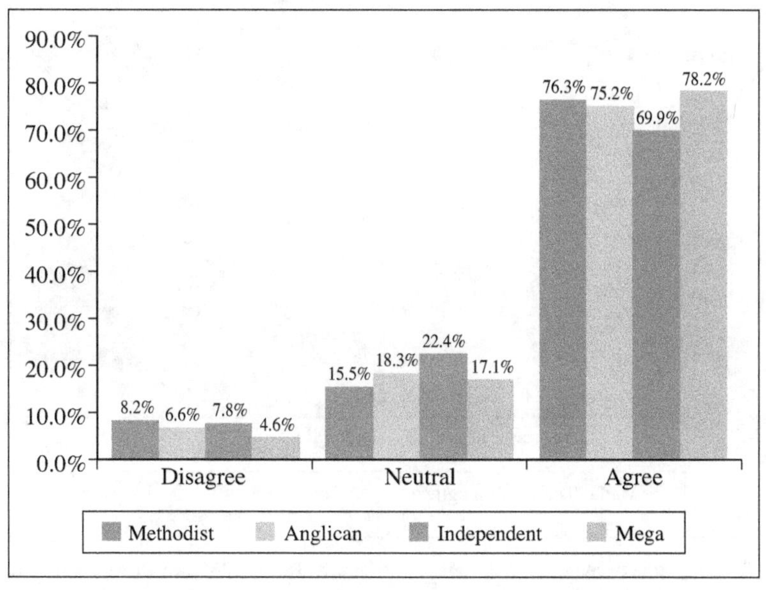

The relation between the variables is significant, X^2 (8, N = 2656) = 19.673, p = .012.

174. H2.9 *Christians should interact more with non-Christians.*

The majority of respondents across denominations agreed with this statement (see Figure H2.9). The

Figure H2.9

Belief that Christians should Interact More with non-Christians According to Denomination

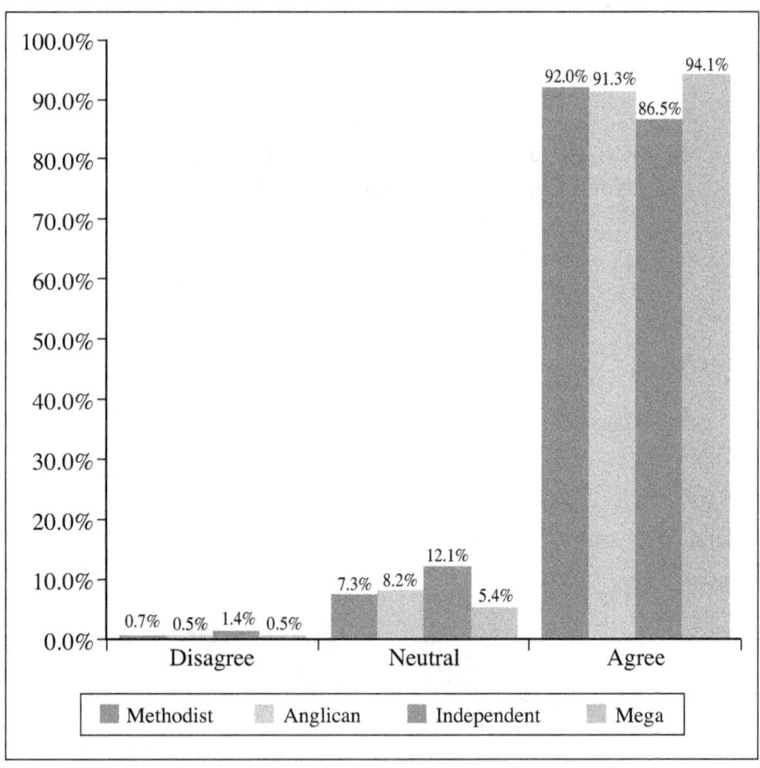

The relation between the variables is significant, X^2 (8, N = 2658) = 25.202, p = .001.

findings were similar across ages and education. While this broad agreement is not unusual in a society with a strong multicultural ethos, the two statements below show some variation between the mainline and megachurch respondents in terms of social habits.

175. H3.1 *I have friends from the following different religions.*

Megachurch respondents were more likely to have friends from different religions (see Figure H3.1). There may be two reasons for this. Firstly, they are more likely to have come from Buddhist or Taoist backgrounds themselves; secondly, the "seeker church" orientation of megachurches encourages them to socialize with non-Christians.

176. H3.2 *I spend most of my leisure and social activities with my following friends.*

Megachurch respondents are (marginally) more likely to spend time with friends from different religions than respondents from other denominations (see Figure H3.2). Again, this is probably because they are more likely to have come from Buddhist or Taoist backgrounds themselves; and the "seeker church" orientation of megachurches encourages them to socialize with non-Christians.

Figure H3.1
Friends from the Following Different Religions According to Denomination

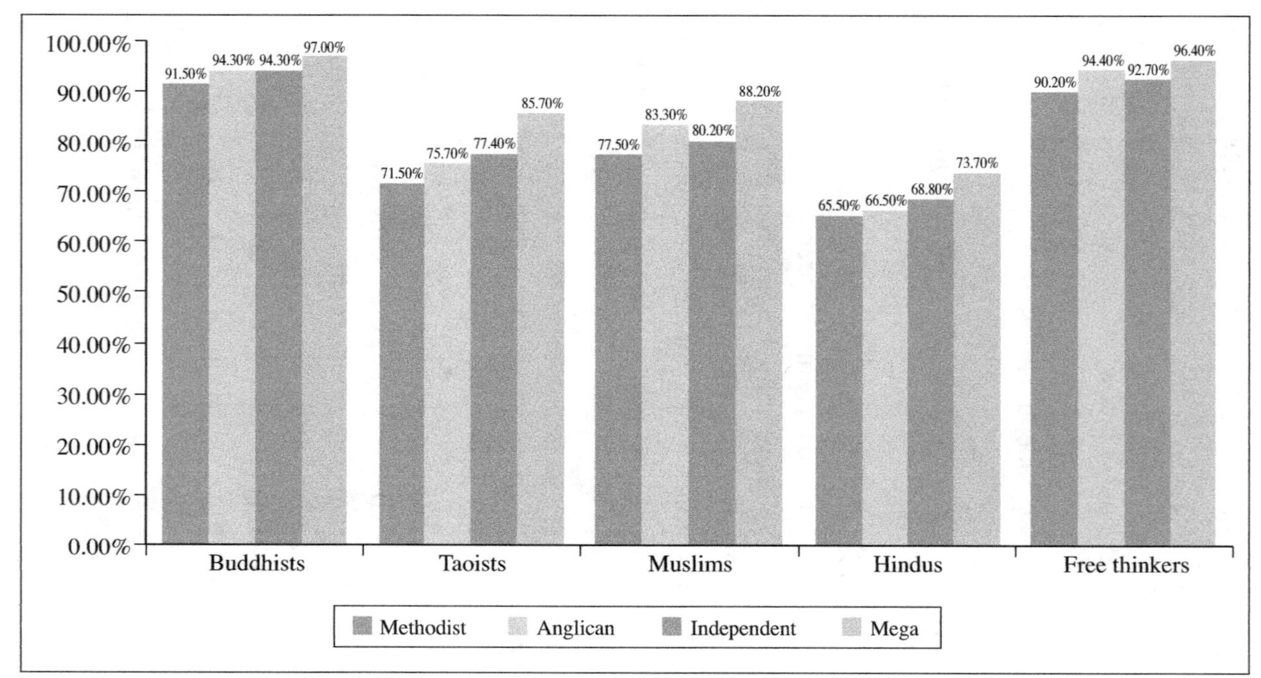

Figure H3.2
Leisure and Social Activities with Following Friends According to Denomination

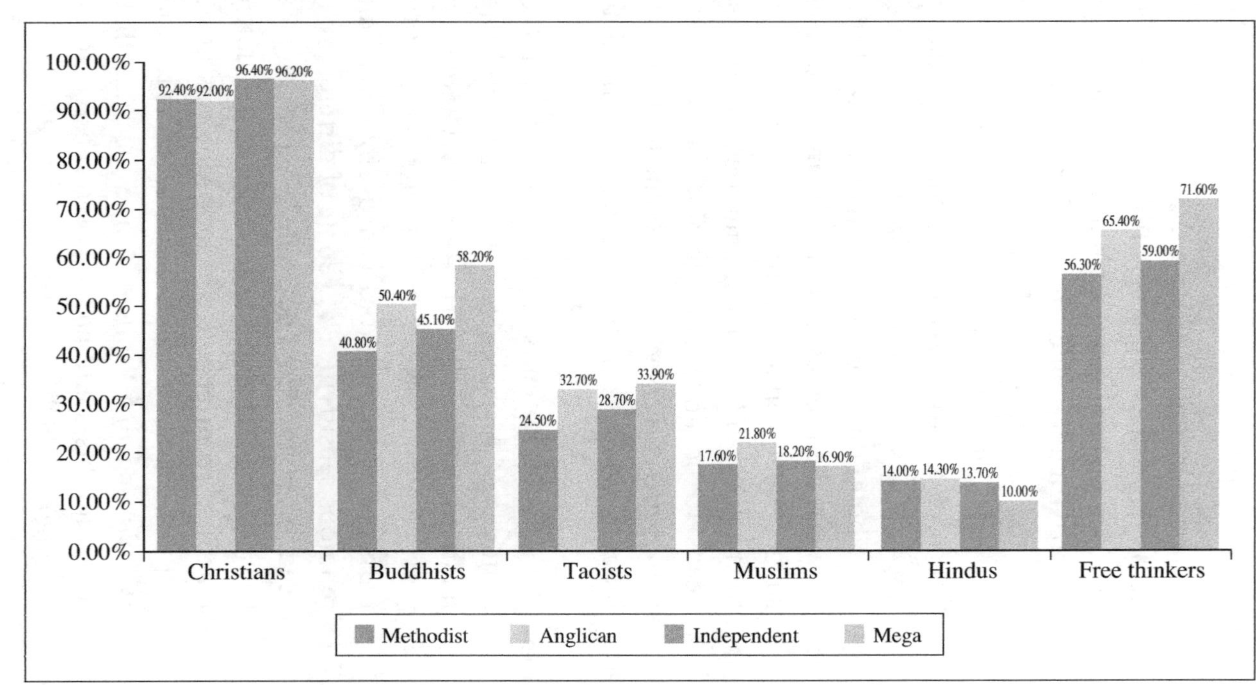

Conclusion

177. Just under half of respondents "agreed" that Christian values are compatible with other ethnic, cultural and religious communities in Singapore. Approximately one third of respondents were "neutral" on the matter. This high portion of "neutral" answers could be either because respondents do not have a strong opinion or that they may prefer not to register a positive or negative answer. On the whole, this suggests a perception of distinction between themselves and other communities. It also suggests a perception of difference in values between themselves and other communities. More research needs to be undertaken to find out exactly what values are perceived to be incompatible and if such incompatibility can be reconciled or mediated.

178. Several statements were made to gauge the attitudes of respondents towards proselytizing in a multicultural society (H2.4–H2.8). The majority of respondents across denominations "agreed" that "the message of God's Word can overcome ethnic and religious sensitivities"; "people of different religions need to hear the Word of God"; "God has commanded Christians to evangelize to everyone"; "unfriendly reactions from people of other religions are God's test of Christians' perseverance in spreading his Word"; and that "spreading the message that God loves all his children is not offensive to people of other faiths".

179. At first glance, such findings may suggest that respondents are less than sensitive to the beliefs of other faiths when it comes to proselytizing. Such an interpretation would be of concern in a multicultural and multireligious society like Singapore. Indeed, there may even have been controversial incidents reported in the media that serve to confirm such an interpretation of the findings.[8] After all, the combined belief that God's Word can overcome religious sensitivities, and that people of different religions need to hear the Word of God, would result in a predictable reaction from other faith communities.

180. We followed up on these findings in the post-survey focus group interviews. They sought to contextualize the findings with qualitative feedback from respondents. All the respondents affirmed that they "agreed" with the statements above. However when asked to elaborate, they made qualifications such as "I'll only do it [evangelize] if the setting is right"; "Of course, I won't evangelize to a Muslim or someone whom I think is not receptive"; "We have to be sensitive to the setting"; "We can't just go up to a stranger and say 'do you want to accept Christ or not?' It's not going to work". The post-survey focus group interviews found that there was a strong acknowledgement of Singapore's multicultural and multireligious complexion among respondents.

181. As such, the survey findings and focus group interviews suggest that there is a clear difference between *conviction* and *follow-up action*. The former does not automatically lead to the latter. The majority of respondents show strong conviction over the need to spread God's Word and to reach out to the unconverted ("The Great Commission" as one respondent put it). This is consistent with biblical teachings and the evangelical ethos present in many denominations. Furthermore, the high level of respondents' conviction on the need to proselytize may be a clear statement of their beliefs.

182. However, the respondents' actions may not always be consistent with this conviction. Respondents may hesitate or refrain from acting out fully their convictions for a variety of reasons. The socialization process where state institutions, national education and government discourse have reinforced the message of the importance of religious harmony through the decades may have resulted in respondents mediating their actions to match social and cultural norms. In addition, respondents are reflexive agents who are able to rationally distinguish between private conviction and the possible ramifications of conviction-led actions. In such cases there is little follow-up action to this conviction.

183. Nevertheless, there may be follow-up action but only after respondents have adapted such actions to the realities of the local multicultural setting. This type of *strategic proselytization* is observed in three forms. Firstly, a "friendship first" approach where respondents may first befriend would-be converts before proselytizing. As one respondent remarked "it is part of our 'caring system' where we show care and friendship first. We get to know them as real people first". Here, respondents show interest in the personal lives of non-believers, as well as to provide social support, instead of viewing them as digits for conversion in the belief that this would make God's Word more meaningful and authentic.[9]

184. Secondly, a "blessed persona" approach where the Christian's personal life testimony is offered as an example of God's blessing in order to reach out to non-believers. By re-telling how one overcomes personal obstacles and dilemmas, the respondent becomes a vivid demonstration of divine forgiveness, inclusion and happiness, thus making the abstract message of God's Word a tangible attraction for non-believers. In such cases, respondents hold themselves up to be role models or representatives of Christ who pique the curiosity of non-believers. One respondent recounted, "people have asked me why I'm so happy, what secret do I have? Then I tell them". This is consistent with the broader literature that notes how megachurches "tend to emphasize the personalistic aspects of faith — a believer's personal relationship with Jesus and the ways in which faith can help individuals address numerous domestic and personal issues in order to demonstrate that Christianity is relevant" (Ellingson 2010, p. 251; see also Sargeant 2000).

185. Thirdly, through "opportune" approach where respondents await the right opportunity to proselytize. Here, respondents approach people who they are familiar with such as fellow students or co-workers whom they think may be receptive to their message. They could be people facing personal crisis, looking for meaning in life or whom they believe are ready to hear the message. In such cases, respondents rely on their own discretion and timing. One respondent remarked "if they are Godless but happy, [I have] no problem! If they resist [the message of God] because they are down and unhappy, then wait for a while".

186. The findings and subsequent interviews suggest a healthy tension between conviction and follow-up action. As we have seen, recent high profile cases show that there are times when conviction does lead to follow-up action. More research needs to be conducted into what causes this tension to disappear and how to ensure that the sensitivity to the beliefs of other faith communities remains an integral part of this tension. Conversely it is also important to study how the more strongly evangelical elements in the Christian community view the general gap between conviction and follow-up action. Do they see it as an acceptable compromise for living in a multicultural society or do they view it as a failure to carry out God's work?

187. The majority of respondents across denominations "agreed" that Christians should interact more with non-Christians. However, the survey found that megachurch respondents were more likely to have friends from other religions, especially those from the Buddhist and Taoist community, as well as more likely to spend their leisure time with them. This may be due to two factors. Firstly megachurch respondents are more likely to have parents of Buddhist or Taoist backgrounds. Secondly, the "seeker church" orientation of megachurches encourages their members to socialize with non-Christians, thus minimizing the distance between the church and the unconverted.

NOTES

1. The Singapore middle class has been generally defined with two modes of analysis — class stratification (Tan 2005; Quah et al 1991); and consumption patterns (Chua and Tan 1999). Both modes of analysis may be deployed in a complementary fashion. Tan (2005, p. 11) uses the monthly household median income as a dividing line between working and middle class households, which was S$3,638 in 2000, and S$5,000 in 2010 (Department of Statistics 2011).
2. The census figures in this section are of "Other Christians" (non-Catholics). Source: *Census of Population 2010: Statistical Release 1 Demographic Characteristics, Education, Language and Religion*. Singapore: Singapore Department of Statistics, 2010.
3. While the youngest group in the Census 2010 is 15–29 years, the survey respondents are grouped as 18–29 years.
4. Public housing refers to Housing and Development Board apartments.
5. Private housing refers to both landed property and private apartments/condominiums
6. The term "compatible" was left open to respondents' own interpretation as the statement sought to gauge their perception of other communities.
7. The "Great Commission" is interpreted as Jesus Christ's instructions to his disciples to spread the Gospel to the world. It is usually taken to mean missionary work, evangelism, and baptism. A popular reading of the "Great Commission" comes from Matthew 28:16–20.
8. *Channel News Asia*, "Pastor's comments on Buddhism/ Taoism 'inappropriate & unacceptable': MHA", 8 February 2010; "Duo charged under Sedition Act", *Straits Times*, 15 April 2008.

9. One respondent was proselytized to in this manner. She was from a dysfunctional family and found “acceptance” among her Christian friends, which made her more “open to God’s message”.

REFERENCES

Berger, Peter L., ed. *The Desecularisation of the World*. Grand Rapids: Eerdmans, 1999.

Bourdieu, Pierre. *Distinction: A Social Critique of the Judgement of Taste*, translated by Richard Nice. London: Routledge, 2002 (1979).

______. "The Forms of Capital". In *Handbook of Theory and Research for the Sociology of Education*, edited by John G. Richardson. New York: Greenwood Press, 1986.

Bourdieu, Pierre and Jean-Claude Passeron. *Reproduction in Education, Society and Culture*. London; Beverly Hills: Sage Publications, 1977.

Bramadat, Paul and David Seljak, eds. *Christianity and Ethnicity in Canada*. Toronto: Toronto University Press, 2008.

Bruce, Steve. "Secularisation". In *The New Blackwell Companion to the Sociology of Religion*, edited by Bryan S. Turner. Oxford: Wiley-Blackwell, 2010.

______. *God is Dead: Secularisation in the West*. Oxford: Blackwell Publishing, 2002.

______. *Pray TV: Televangelism in America*. London: Routledge, 1990.

Chew, Phyllis Ghim-Lian. "Remaking Singapore: Language, Culture, and Identity in a Globalized World". In *Language Policy, Culture, and Identity in Asian Contexts*, edited by Amy B.M. Tsui and James W. Tollefson. New Jersey: Lawrence Erlbaum Associates, 2007.

Chong, Terence. "Filling the Moral Void: The Christian Right and the State in Singapore". *Journal of Contemporary Asia* 41, no. 4 (2011): 566–83.

Chua, Beng Huat and Tan Joo Ean. "Singapore: Where the new middle class sets the standard". In *Culture and Privilege in Capitalist Asia*, edited by Michael Pinches. London and New York: Routledge, 1999.

Clammer, John R. *The Social Structure of Religion: A Sociological Study of Christianity in Singapore*. Singapore: Department of Sociology, University of Singapore, 1978.

Coleman, Simon. *The Globalisation of Charismatic Christianity: Spreading the Gospel of Prosperity*. Cambridge: Cambridge University Press, 2000.

______. "Conservative Protestantism and the World Order: The Faith Movement in the United States and Sweden". *Sociology of Religion* 54, no. 4 (1993): 353–73.

Cox, Harvey. *Fire from Heaven: The Rise of Pentecostal Spirituality and the Reshaping of Religion in the 21st Century*. Jackson TN: Da Capo Press, 2001.

Department of Statistics. "Key Household Income Trends, 2010". Singapore, 2011.

Elisha, Omri. "Sins of Our Soccer Moms: Servant Evangelism and the Spiritual Injuries of Class". In *Local Actions: Cultural Activism, Power, and Public Life in America*, edited by Melissa Checker and Margaret Fishman. New York: Columbia University Press, 2004.

Ellingson, Stephen. "New Research on Megachurches: Non-denominationalism and Sectarianism". In *The New Blackwell Companion to the Sociology of Religion*, edited by Bryan S. Turner. Oxford: Wiley-Blackwell, 2010.

______. *The Megachurch and the Mainline: Remaking Religious Tradition in the Twenty-First Century*. Chicago: University of Chicago Press, 2007.

Ester, Peter, Loek Halman, Ruud de Moor. *The Individualizing Society: Value Change in Europe and North America*. Tilburg: Tilburg University Press, 1994.

Goh, Daniel P.S. "State and Social Christianity in Post-colonial Singapore". *Sojourn: Journal of Social Issues in Southeast Asia* 25, no. 1 (2010): 54–89.

Goh, Robbie B.H. "Hillsong and 'Megachurch' Practice: Semiotics, Spatial Logic and the Embodiment of Contemporary Evangelical Protestantism". *Material Religion* 4, no. 3 (2008): 284–305.

Hill, Michael and Lian Kwen Fee. *The Politics of Nation-building and Citizenship in Singapore*. London and New York: Routledge, 1995.

Hollinger, Dennis. "Enjoying God Forever: A Historical/Sociological Profile of the Health and Wealth Gospel in the U.S.A". In *Religion and Power, Decline and Growth: Sociological Analyses of Religion in Britain, Poland and the Americas*, edited by Peter Gee and John Fulton. London: British Sociological Association, 1991.

Kwok, Kian-Woon. "Chinese-Education Intellectuals in Singapore: Marginality, Memory and Modernity". *Asian Journal of Social Science* 29, no. 3 (2001): 495–519.

Lee, Siew Hua and Susan Long. "The Rise of the Megachurch: Gospel & Glitz". *Straits Times*, 17 July 2010.

Martin, David. *The Theory of Secularisation*. Oxford: Blackwell Press, 1978.

Mathews, Mathew. "Christianity in Singapore: The Voice of Moral Conscience to the State". *Journal of Contemporary Religion* 24, no. 1 (2009): 53–65.

Miller, Donald E. *Reinventing American Protestantism: Christianity in the New Millennium*. California: University of California Press, 1997.

Ong, Sor Fern. "Rise of New Churches". *Straits Times*, 21 July 2008.

Pereira, Alexius A. "Religiosity and Economic Development in Singapore". *Journal of Contemporary Religion* 20, no. 2 (2005): 161–77.

Putnam, Robert D. and David E. Campbell. *American Grace: How Religion Divides and Unites Us*. New York: Simon & Schuster, 2010.

Quah, Stella et al. *Social Class in Singapore*. Singapore. National University Press, 1991.

Sargeant, Kimon Howland. *Seeker Churches: Promoting Traditional Religion in Non-Traditional Way*. New Brunswick: Rutgers University Press, 2000.

Sng, Bobby E.K. and You Poh Seng. *Religious Trends in Singapore with special reference to Christianity*. Singapore: Graduates' Christian Fellowship and Fellowship of Evangelical Students, 1982.

Tan, Ern Ser. *Does Class Matter: Social Stratification and Orientations in Singapore*. Singapore: World Scientific, 2005.

Thumma, Scott and Warren Bird. "Changes in American Megachurches: Tracing Eight Years of Growth and Innovation in the Nation's Largest-Attendance Congregations". Hartford Institution for Region Research, 2008. <http://hirr.hartsem.edu/megachurch/Changes%20in%20American%20Megachurches%20Sept%2012%202008.pdf> (accessed 25 July 2011).

Thumma, Scott and Dave Travis. *Beyond Megachurch Myths: What We Can Learn from America's Largest Churches*. San Francisco: John Wiley & Sons, 2007.

Tong, Joy Kooi Chin. "McDonaldisation and the Megachurch: A Case Study of City Harvest Church, Singapore". In *Religious Commodification in Asia*, editied by Pattana Kitiarsa. New York: Routledge, 2008.

Turner, Bryan S. "Religion in a Post-secular Society". In *The New Blackwell Companion to the Sociology of Religion*, edited by Bryan S. Turner. Oxford: Wiley-Blackwell, 2010.

Twitchell, James B *Branded Nation*. New York: Simon and Schuster, 2004.

Weber, Max. *From Max Weber: Essays in Sociology*, edited by H.H. Gerth and C. Wright Mills. London: Routledge, 1991 [1948].

ANNEX ONE

A Survey of Church-Going Protestants in Singapore

Instructions:

This survey consists of 8 sections.

Kindly answer all questions.

Do not hesitate to ask for clarification.

For official use only:

Date	
Ref. No.	
Church Code.	

Bio-data:

Name: (Optional) ____________________

Gender: 1. ☐ Male 2. ☐ Female

Nationality: 1. ☐ Singaporean 2. ☐ Permanent Resident,

specify nationality: ____________________

3. ☐ Foreigner,

specify nationality: ____________________

Ethnic Group: 1. ☐ Chinese 2. ☐ Malay 3. ☐ Indian

4. ☐ Eurasian 5. ☐ Others, specify: ____________________

Age: __________

Marital Status: 1. ☐ Single 2. ☐ Married

3. ☐ Divorced/Separated 4. ☐ Widowed

Section A: Socio-economic and Cultural Background

A1. What is the highest level of education that you have attained?

1. ☐ No formal qualification e.g. lower Primary, Best 1–3
2. ☐ Primary e.g. PSLE, Best 4
3. ☐ Lower secondary e.g. ITE Basic, WISE 1-3
4. ☐ Secondary e.g. “O” or “N” Levels, NTC Grade 3
5. ☐ Upper secondary i.e. “A” Levels
6. ☐ Upper secondary e.g. Vocational, NTC Grades 1 & 2
7. ☐ Polytechnic diploma
8. ☐ Professional qualification and other diplomas
9. ☐ University first degree
10. ☐ University postgraduate diploma or degree
11. ☐ Others, please specify ____________________

A2. What is your occupational group?

1. ☐ Legislators, Senior Officials & Managers, including Businessmen
2. ☐ Professionals, please specify ____________________
3. ☐ Associate Professionals & Technicians

4. ☐ Clerical Workers
5. ☐ Service & Sales Workers
6. ☐ Agricultural & Fishery Workers
7. ☐ Production Craftsmen & Related Workers
8. ☐ Plant & Machine Operators & Assemblers
9. ☐ Cleaners, Labourers & Related Workers
10. ☐ Others, please specify ____________________
11. ☐ Retired, please specify previous occupation ____________________

A3. What is your gross monthly *personal* income?

1. ☐ No income	2. ☐ Below $1,000
3. ☐ $1,000 to $1,499	4. ☐ $1,500 to $1,999
5. ☐ $2,000 to $2,999	6. ☐ $3,000 to $3,999
7. ☐ $4,000 to $4,999	8. ☐ $5,000 to $5,999
9. ☐ $6,000 to $6,999	10. ☐ $7,000 to $7,999
11. ☐ $8,000 to $8,999	12. ☐ $9,000 to $9,999
13. ☐ $10,000 and above	

A4. What is your gross monthly *household* income, i.e. the combined income of your family?

1. ☐ Below S$1,000
2. ☐ $1,000 to $1,499
3. ☐ $1,500 to $1,999
4. ☐ $2,000 to $2,999
5. ☐ $3,000 to $3,999
6. ☐ $4,000 to $4,999
7. ☐ $5,000 to $5,999
8. ☐ $6,000 to $6,999
9. ☐ $7,000 to $7,999
10. ☐ $8,000 to $8,999
11. ☐ $9,000 to $9,999
12. ☐ $10,000 and above

A5. What language(s) did you use at home before the age of 18?

You can choose more than one

1. ☐ English
2. ☐ Mandarin
3. ☐ Malay
4. ☐ Tamil
5. ☐ Other languages and dialects (e.g. Hokkien, Urdu etc)

please specify ______________________________

A6. What is your father's highest educational qualification?

1. ☐ No formal schooling
2. ☐ Primary
3. ☐ Secondary
4. ☐ Pre-University
5. ☐ Tertiary, please specify ______________________________

A7. What is your mother's highest educational qualification?

1. ☐ No formal schooling　　2. ☐ Primary
3. ☐ Secondary　　4. ☐ Pre-University
5. ☐ Tertiary, please specify ____________

A8. What is/was your father's occupation?

1. ☐ Legislators, Senior Officials & Managers, including Businessmen
2. ☐ Professionals, please specify ____________
3. ☐ Associate Professionals & Technicians
4. ☐ Clerical Workers
5. ☐ Service & Sales Workers
6. ☐ Agricultural & Fishery Workers
7. ☐ Production Craftsmen & Related Workers
8. ☐ Plant & Machine Operators & Assemblers
9. ☐ Cleaners, Labourers & Related Workers
10. ☐ Others, please specify ____________

A9. What is/was your mother's occupation?

1. ☐ Legislators, Senior Officials & Managers, including Businessmen
2. ☐ Professionals, please specify ____________________
3. ☐ Associate Professionals & Technicians
4. ☐ Clerical Workers
5. ☐ Service & Sales Workers
6. ☐ Agricultural & Fishery Workers
7. ☐ Production Craftsmen & Related Workers
8. ☐ Plant & Machine Operators & Assemblers
9. ☐ Cleaners, Labourers & Related Workers
10. ☐ Others, please specify ____________________

A10. Please list the schools you have attended at the primary, secondary and pre-university levels and the schools' religious affiliations, if any.

Level	**School**	**Religious affiliation**
		E.g. Buddhist, Methodist…
______	______	______
______	______	______
______	______	______
______	______	______
______	______	______

A11. What kind of housing did you stay the longest before the age of 18?

1. ☐ HDB 1–2 Room
2. ☐ HDB 3-Room
3. ☐ HDB 4-Room
4. ☐ HDB 5-Room/Executive/Masionette/HUDC
5. ☐ Bungalow/Semi-D/Terrace
6. ☐ Private apartment/Condominium
7. ☐ Others, please specify ______

A12. What kind of housing are you staying in now?

1 ☐ HDB 1–2 Room
2 ☐ HDB 3-Room
3 ☐ HDB 4-Room
4 ☐ HDB 5-Room/Executive/Masionette/HUDC
5. ☐ Bungalow/Semi-D/Terrace
6. ☐ Private apartment/Condominium
7. ☐ Others, please specify ____________________

A13 Are any of your following family members Christians?

a. Father 1. ☐ Yes 2. ☐ No 3. ☐ Don't know

ii) If yes, did he become a Christian before you?

1. ☐ Yes 2. ☐ No

b. Mother 1. ☐ Yes 2. ☐ No 3. ☐ Don't know

ii) If yes, did she become a Christian before you?

1. ☐ Yes 2. ☐ No

c. Siblings 1. ☐ Yes 2. ☐ No 3. ☐ Not applicable

d. Spouse 1. ☐ Yes 2. ☐ No 3. ☐ Not applicable

e. Children 1. ☐ Yes 2. ☐ No 3. ☐ Not applicable

A14. Do any of the following family members attend the same church as you?

a. Father 1. ☐ Yes 2. ☐ No 3. ☐ Not applicable

b. Mother 1. ☐ Yes 2. ☐ No 3. ☐ Not applicable

c. Siblings 1. ☐ Yes 2. ☐ No 3. ☐ Not applicable

d. Spouse 1. ☐ Yes 2. ☐ No 3. ☐ Not applicable

e. Children 1. ☐ Yes 2. ☐ No 3. ☐ Not applicable

Section B: Reasons for Attending This Church

B1.1 Which year did you become a Christian?

Year: ____________________

B1.2 Where did you converted?

1. ☐ I was born into a Christian family
2. ☐ At my current church
3. ☐ At another church
4. ☐ At a mass evangelistic rally
5. ☐ Through parachurch organizations e.g. Varsity Christian Fellowship, Youth For Christ, etc
6. ☐ Others, please specify ____________________

B2. Is your current church the first church you have attended since you became a Christian?

1. ☐ Yes
2. ☐ No

If not, please provide a list of churches you have regularly attended (for at least six months) since you became a Christian.

Year	**Name of church**
E.g. 1988–1990	
____________	______________________________
____________	______________________________
____________	______________________________

On a scale of 1 to 5 (1 – Strongly Disagree; 3 – Neutral; 5 – Strongly Agree), to what extent do you disagree or agree with the following statements?

Please circle the number that reflects your choice.

I am attending this church because…	**Strongly Disagree**	**Disagree**	**Neutral**	**Agree**	**Strongly Agree**
B3.1 … I have always attended this church.	1	2	3	4	5
B3.2 … I like the preaching.	1	2	3	4	5
B3.3 … the teachings are doctrinally sound.	1	2	3	4	5
B3.4 … of the small group ministry.	1	2	3	4	5

On a scale of 1 to 5 (1 – Strongly Disagree; 3 – Neutral; 5 – Strongly Agree), to what extent do you disagree or agree with the following statements?

Please circle the number that reflects your choice.

I am attending this church because…		Strongly Disagree	Disagree	Neutral	Agree	Strongly Agree
B3.5	… I have made good friends here.	1	2	3	4	5
B3.6	… I like the activities/programmes of this church.	1	2	3	4	5
B3.7	… I have a deeper experience of God here.	1	2	3	4	5
B3.8	… I feel the Word of God is lived out here.	1	2	3	4	5
B3.9	… I feel that the people in this church care for me.	1	2	3	4	5
B3.10	… I like the praise & worship sessions.	1	2	3	4	5
B3.11	… my parent(s) attend this church.	1	2	3	4	5
B3.12	… it is an exciting church.	1	2	3	4	5
B3.13	… it is a big church.	1	2	3	4	5

B4. How often do you participate in the activities of this church, e.g. worship service, prayer meeting, Bible study, etc…?

1. ☐ Less than once a month
2. ☐ One–three times a month
3. ☐ Once a week
4. ☐ Two–three times a week
5. ☐ Four times or more a week

Section C: Money and Finance

C1. On average, how would you allocate your income according to the following five categories?

_____ % giving to church (e.g. tithes, offering, missions, building fund etc) and other Christian organizations (e.g. parachurches, missions organizations etc)

_____ % savings e.g. insurance, regular savings, education fund etc

_____ % personal expenses e.g. clothes, dining, entertainment & leisure activities/hobbies etc

_____ % family expenses e.g. household bills, money for parents, medical etc

_____ % others

On a scale of 1 to 5 (1 – Strongly Disagree; 3 – Neutral; 5 – Strongly Agree), to what extent do you disagree or agree with the following statements?

Please circle the number that reflects your choice.

		Strongly Disagree	**Disagree**	**Neutral**	**Agree**	**Strongly Agree**
C2.1	Money is important to me.	1	2	3	4	5
C2.2	It is important that I should work hard to earn a high income.	1	2	3	4	5
C2.3	Giving to my church is a form of duty.	1	2	3	4	5

C2.4	By giving to my church I can expect God to bless me spiritually.	1	2	3	4	5
C2.5	By giving to my church I can expect God to bless me materially.	1	2	3	4	5
C2.6	It is important that my church uses my offering to spread God's Word.	1	2	3	4	5
C2.7	Pastors and church leaders today need to show leadership qualities like CEOs of companies.	1	2	3	4	5
C2.8	It is important that my church grows in congregation size over the years.	1	2	3	4	5
C2.9	The financial growth of my church is a sign of God's blessing over it.	1	2	3	4	5
C2.10	All full-time staff (e.g. pastors, church workers, counsellors, etc) should be paid market-competitive salaries.	1	2	3	4	5
C2.11	The salaries of pastors and church leaders should be in keeping with the size of their congregation or flock.	1	2	3	4	5

		Strongly Disagree	Disagree	Neutral	Agree	Strongly Agree
C2.12	I trust my church to deal with its finances honestly.	1	2	3	4	5
C2.13	I trust my church to deal with its finances effectively.	1	2	3	4	5
C2.14	If I am a faithful Christian, God will bless me with prosperity.	1	2	3	4	5
C2.15	Christians are entitled to spend what they earn on what they want.	1	2	3	4	5
C2.16	Christians should give a sizeable part of their earnings to God.	1	2	3	4	5
C2.17	Christians should save a sizeable part of their earnings.	1	2	3	4	5

Section D: Religiosity

D1. How often do you read the Bible?

1. ☐ At least once a day
2. ☐ At least 2–3 times a week
3. ☐ Once a week
4. ☐ Once a month
5. ☐ Seldom

D2. How often do you read other religious books or literature (including online materials)?

1. ☐ At least once a day
2. ☐ At least 2–3 times a week
3. ☐ Once a week
4. ☐ Once a month
5. ☐ Seldom

D3. How often do you pray (apart from giving thanks during meals)?

1. ☐ At least once a day
2. ☐ At least 2–3 times a week
3. ☐ Once a week
4. ☐ Once a month
5. ☐ Seldom

Section E: Politics

On a scale of 1 to 5 (1 – Strongly Disagree; 3 – Neutral; 5 – Strongly Agree), to what extent do you disagree or agree with the following statements?

Please circle the number that reflects your choice.

		Strongly Disagree	Disagree	Neutral	Agree	Strongly Agree
E1.1	The religion of a political candidate or government leader is important to me.	1	2	3	4	5
E1.2	It is according to God's Will that our present government is in place.	1	2	3	4	5
E1.3	It is our duty as Christians to pray for a wise and righteous government.	1	2	3	4	5
E1.4	It is important to have as many Christians serving in government as possible.	1	2	3	4	5
E1.5	All things being equal, Christians make better government leaders than people of *no* religion.	1	2	3	4	5
E1.6	All things being equal, Christians make better government leaders than people of *other* religions.	1	2	3	4	5

On a scale of 1 to 5 (1 – Strongly Disagree; 3 – Neutral; 5 – Strongly Agree), to what extent do you disagree or agree with the following statements?

Please circle the number that reflects your choice.

		Strongly Disagree	Disagree	Neutral	Agree	Strongly Agree
E1.7	All things being equal, people with religion make better government leaders than people with no religion.	1	2	3	4	5
E1.8	Christians in government should pray and read the Scriptures for wisdom over public policy matters.	1	2	3	4	5
E1.9	Christians in government should prioritize the Will of God and Scripture teachings in public policy matters.	1	2	3	4	5
E1.10	Christians in government can adequately represent or take care of communities of different faiths.	1	2	3	4	5
E2.1	My Christian values influence my views on public policy issues (e.g. casinos, abortion).	1	2	3	4	5
E2.2	It is sometimes necessary to accept public policies which may run counter to Christian values (e.g. casinos, abortion).	1	2	3	4	5

		Strongly Disagree	Disagree	Neutral	Agree	Strongly Agree
E2.3	Christians should collectively express their views on public policy issues in public.	1	2	3	4	5
E2.4	It is acceptable to support Christians active in causes or issues that are not church-related (e.g. casinos, abortion).	1	2	3	4	5
E2.5	It is acceptable for my pastor to comment on civil society or public policy matters over the pulpit or during church service.	1	2	3	4	5
E3.1	The Singapore government is becoming too liberal in terms of moral values.	1	2	3	4	5
E3.2	When it comes to public policies, the Singapore government is more concerned with economic benefits than with moral values.	1	2	3	4	5

Section F: Self-perceptions of Religious Identity

On a scale of 1 to 5 (1 – Strongly Disagree; 3 – Neutral; 5 – Strongly Agree), to what extent do you disagree or agree with the following statements?

Please circle the number that reflects your choice.

		Strongly Disagree	Disagree	Neutral	Agree	Strongly Agree
F1.1	Singapore society is losing its moral values.	1	2	3	4	5
F1.2	Religious teachings are essential to preserve the moral values of our society.	1	2	3	4	5
F1.3	Some sections of the Christian community in Singapore are becoming too morally permissive.	1	2	3	4	5
F1.4	Some sections of the Christian community in Singapore are straying too far from Scriptural teachings (Bible).	1	2	3	4	5
F1.5	Some sections of the Christian community in Singapore are too morally conservative.	1	2	3	4	5
F1.6	Some sections of the Christian community in Singapore are interpreting the Bible too literally.	1	2	3	4	5

		Strongly Disagree	Disagree	Neutral	Agree	Strongly Agree
F1.7	The Christian community in Singapore has been under close political and public scrutiny lately.	1	2	3	4	5
F1.8	Christians in Singapore are often perceived to be religiously intolerant.	1	2	3	4	5
F2.1	I believe we are living in the "end times" as prophesized in the Bible.	1	2	3	4	5
F2.2	I believe that my generation will witness the second coming of Jesus Christ.	1	2	3	4	5
F2.3	Natural disasters such as earthquakes and tsunamis are sent from God to punish unrepentant sinners.	1	2	3	4	5

Section G: Sex and Sexuality

On a scale of 1 to 5 (1 – Strongly Disagree; 3 – Neutral; 5 – Strongly Agree), to what extent do you disagree or agree with the following statements?

Please circle the number that reflects your choice.

		Strongly Disagree	Disagree	Neutral	Agree	Strongly Agree
G1.1	Pre-marital sex (sex before marriage) is fine as long as those involved are consenting adults and if they practise safe sex.	1	2	3	4	5
G1.2	Under no circumstance should a person have sex with another person's wife/husband.	1	2	3	4	5
G1.3	It is morally wrong to engage in homosexuality (same sex sexual relations).	1	2	3	4	5
G1.4	I feel comfortable interacting with homosexuals.	1	2	3	4	5
G1.5	I do not mind making friends with homosexuals.	1	2	3	4	5
G1.6	I do not mind a homosexual family member.	1	2	3	4	5
G1.7	I do not mind a homosexual church leader.	1	2	3	4	5

		Strongly Disagree	Disagree	Neutral	Agree	Strongly Agree
G1.8	If I found out that a Christian I know is a homosexual, I will try to use the Scriptures to encourage him/her to change his/her sexual orientation.	1	2	3	4	5
G1.9	Homosexual activities should be discouraged through laws such as Section 377A of the Penal Code (which provides for a jail sentence of up to two years should a man be found to have committed an act of "gross indecency" with another man).	1	2	3	4	5
G1.10	Homosexuality is wrong because the Scriptures say it is wrong.	1	2	3	4	5

G2.1 Do you have friends who are homosexuals? 1. ☐ Yes 2. ☐ No

G2.2 Do you go out with friends who are homosexuals? 1. ☐ Yes 2. ☐ No

G2.3 Do you have family members who are homosexuals? 1. ☐ Yes 2. ☐ No

G2.4 Do you know Christians who are homosexuals? 1. ☐ Yes 2. ☐ No

On a scale of 1 to 5 (1 – Strongly Disagree; 3 – Neutral; 5 – Strongly Agree), to what extent do you disagree or agree with the following statements?

Please circle the number that reflects your choice.

		Strongly Disagree	Disagree	Neutral	Agree	Strongly Agree
G3.1	Abortion is morally wrong.	1	2	3	4	5
G3.2	Abortion should be made illegal in Singapore.	1	2	3	4	5
G4.1	The use of contraceptives is morally wrong. (Contraceptives include condoms, female condoms, and birth control pills)	1	2	3	4	5
G4.2	Contraceptives should be made illegal in Singapore.	1	2	3	4	5
G5.1	Sex education in Singapore schools today is too liberal.	1	2	3	4	5
G5.2	Sex education should incorporate more moral or religious values.	1	2	3	4	5
G5.3	Sex education should teach only abstinence (no sex before marriage).	1	2	3	4	5

		Strongly Disagree	Disagree	Neutral	Agree	Strongly Agree
G5.4	Sex education should teach both abstinence and the use of contraceptives.	1	2	3	4	5
G5.5	Teaching students how to use contraceptives will encourage them to have pre-marital sex.	1	2	3	4	5
G5.6	*Not* teaching students how to use contraceptives will *discourage* them from having pre-marital sex.	1	2	3	4	5
G5.7	Sex education should leave out mention of homosexuality (same sex sexual relations).	1	2	3	4	5

G5.8 Sex education should teach that homosexuality is…

Please choose one answer

1. ☐ Morally wrong and unnatural.
2. ☐ Morally acceptable and natural.
3. ☐ Neutral and leave it to the students and parents/religious authorities to decide on whether it is morally acceptable or not.

Section H: Other Religions and Communities

On a scale of 1 to 5 (1 – Strongly Disagree; 3 – Neutral; 5 – Strongly Agree), to what extent do you disagree or agree with the following statements?

Please circle the number that reflects your choice.

		Strongly Disagree	Disagree	Neutral	Agree	Strongly Agree
H1.1	Christian values are compatible with those of different ethnic or cultural communities.	1	2	3	4	5
H1.2	Christian values are compatible with those of different religious communities.	1	2	3	4	5
H2.1	Not believing in God is detrimental to the moral health of Singapore society.	1	2	3	4	5
H2.2	Increasing levels of secularism is not positive for the moral health of Singapore society.	1	2	3	4	5
H2.3	Increasing levels of religiosity (amongst different faiths) is not positive for the moral health of Singapore society.	1	2	3	4	5

		Strongly Disagree	Disagree	Neutral	Agree	Strongly Agree
H2.4	I believe that the message of God's Word can overcome ethnic and religious sensitivities in Singapore.	1	2	3	4	5
H2.5	People of different religions need to hear the Word of God.	1	2	3	4	5
H2.6	I believe God has commanded Christians to evangelize to everyone.	1	2	3	4	5
H2.7	Unfriendly reactions from people of other religions are God's test of Christians' perseverance in spreading his Word.	1	2	3	4	5
H2.8	Spreading the message that God loves all his children is not offensive to non-religious people or people of other faiths.	1	2	3	4	5
H2.9	Christians should interact more with non-Christians.	1	2	3	4	5

H3.1	I have friends from the following different religions: *Please circle those which apply*		Buddhists 1	Taoists 2	Muslims 3	Hindus 4	Free Thinkers 5
H3.2	I spend most of my leisure and social activities with my following friends: *Please circle those which apply*	Christians 1	Buddhists 2	Taoists 3	Muslims 4	Hindus 5	Free Thinkers 6

— End —

Thank you for your participation

INDEX

S

T

ABOUT THE AUTHORS

Terence Chong is a sociologist and Senior Fellow, Institute of Southeast Asian Studies (ISEAS), Singapore. His research interests include cultural policy, religion, and civil society. He is the author of *The Theatre and the State in Singapore: Orthodoxy and Resistance* (2010) and editor of *The AWARE Saga: Civil Society and Public Morality in Singapore* (2011).

Hui Yew-Foong is an anthropologist, Senior Fellow and Coordinator of the Regional Social and Cultural Studies Programme, ISEAS. His research interests include the Chinese minority in Southeast Asia, religion and politics, and cemeteries as heritage sites. He is the author of *Strangers at Home: History and Subjectivity among the Chinese Communities of West Kalimantan, Indonesia* (2011).

www.ingramcontent.com/pod-product-compliance
Lightning Source LLC
LaVergne TN
LVHW050640100826
845148LV00011B/1920

* 9 7 8 9 8 1 4 4 1 4 4 2 5 *